ECONOMIC ANALYSIS OF RICE CULTIVATION

Economic Analysis of Rice Cultivation

A Study of Tamil Nadu

V. Nirmala
Department of Economics
Pondicherry University, Pondicherry

CONCEPT PUBLISHING COMPANY, NEW DELHI 110059

The Indian Council of Social Science Research gave the financial support towards the publication of this work. However, the responsibility for the contents of the book — facts, opinions, conclusion, etc. — is entirely that of the author and not the ICSSR.

ICSSR Consultant : Dr. R. Swarup

ISBN 81-7022-420-9

First Published 1992

Published and Printed by
Ashok Kumar Mittal
Concept Publishing Company
A/15-16, Commercial Block, Mohan Garden
NEW DELHI 110059 (India)

Lasertypeset by
Microtech Advance Printing Systems (Pvt.) Ltd.
H-13, Bali Nagar
NEW DELHI 110015

For

My Guru

Dr. G. Subramaniyan

and

My beloved family members

FOREWORD

The book provides an econometric treatment to various aspects of rice cultivation in the selected study area. Rice being one of the major crops grown in India, the subject selected for investigation assumes great importance in agricultural research. In the study, Dr. V. Nirmala has dealt with some of the vital issues relating to rice cultivation. The objectives of her study have been to examine the cost and return structures, determinants of yield, yield gap and its causes, relationship between farm size and farm efficiency, inequalities in net income distribution, labour absorption and supply response, and economic efficiency of small and large farmer groups growing two popular varieties of rice in Gokilapuram village of Madurai district, Tamil Nadu.

The sampling design adopted to collect data for the study is relevant. The cost and return structure has been studied using the standard procedures, which makes it comparable with other studies. The study points out the various socio-economic and bio-physical factors that inhibit rice cultivation in the study area. The author has been quite successful in using Lau-Yotopaulos profit function approach and Zellner's seemingly unrelated regression technique in examining hypothesis relating to labour absorption, supply response and economic efficiency of farmer groups.

The findings of the study provides useful assessment of the physical and economic performance of the two popular rice varieties. Besides, it also highlights the factors that act as constraint to their expected performance. The study succeeds in providing a number of location-specific suggestions important for policy-making.

On the whole, I am sure that this book would be informative, useful and inspiring to economists, agricultural experts and research students.

Head, Department of
Agricultural Economics,
School of Economics,
Madurai Kamaraj University,
Madurai-625021

Dr. G. SUBRAMANIYAN

ACKNOWLEDGEMENTS

I wish to express my deep sense of gratitude to Dr. G. Subramaniyan, Head, Department of Agricultural Economics, School of Economics, Madurai Kamaraj University, for his expert guidance and invaluable suggestions throughout the study. I am highly indebted to him for the constant encouragement, advice and tireless help extended to me in the realization of my challenge of successfully completing research. It has been an excellent experience working under his efficient supervision.

I acknowledge with pleasure, my profound gratitude to Dr. J.C. Flinn, Agricultural Economist and Head, International Rice Research Institute, Philippines, for his magnanimous help in the computational work. I have also benefited immensely from the invaluable suggestions offered and related literature sent by him on the study. But for his kind assistance, the study would not have been a success.

I am extremely thankful to Dr. R. Sankara Ramalingam, Professor and Head, Madurai Kamaraj University, for his valuable guidance, suggestions and encouragement during the study.

I am highly grateful to Asst. Prof. A. Gunamalai for his tireless assistance, advice and encouragement throughout the work.

I also owe my heart-felt gratitude to Dr. Bandi Kamaiah and Dr. K. Sham Bhat for their encouragement and keen interest in my academic achievements.

My profuse thanks to Asst. Prof. Metilda David and other staff of the Tamil Nadu Agricultural University of Madurai and Coimbatore, officers of the Statistical Offices in the district, taluk and village visited and the respondents, for their kind help, patience and cooperation extended during data collection. I am also thankful to Mr. Nagalingam for assisting me in the work.

I thank the authorities of Madurai Kamaraj University for providing the university fellowship to carry out the research. My thanks are also due to the staff of the Computer Centre for providing me with excellent services in the processing of data.

I also acknowledge with gratitude the financial grant provided by the Indian Council of Social Science Research, New Delhi, for the publication of my thesis.

My special thanks to Mrs. Rajalakshmi Pillai and Prof. V. Sadasivan Pillai for extending their kind cooperation in going through the final manuscript, despite their busy schedule. I also thank Mrs. R.R. Jeyanthi and Mr. K.R. Ravi for typing the script with utmost care and patience.

I am highly indebted to Mrs. Satheswari Subramaniyan, Ms. Karpagavalli, Mr. Palanivel and Ms. Radha Meena for their affectionate and tireless services, interest and encouragement extended, especially during the typing stage.

I am also thankful to my young friends and philosophers Ms. Lumine Dyas, Ms. K. Lakshmi Devi, Mr. S. Nagarajan, Mr. C. Chendroyaperumal, Mr. N. Tamil Selvan, Mr. A. Raja, Mrs. Chellam Subramanian, Mrs. Selvarani Bhaskaran and a host of others unnamed here, for their encouragement, support and advice.

Last but not the least, I owe all my success to my beloved parents, brothers and sisters (MYUR SAGINI), husband and brothers-in-law, who have been my constant source of inspiration, confidence and strength. But for their incessant affection, blessings, advice and encouragement, I would have been nowhere today.

Pondicherry University, Dr. V. NIRMALA
Pondicherry

CONTENTS

Foreword 7
Acknowledgements 9
List of Tables 12
List of Figures 15

1. Introduction 17
2. Gokilapuram: Its Profile, Sample Design and Measurement of Variables 35
3. Concepts and Review of Literature 55
4. Cost and Return Structure 87
5. Determinants of Yield, Yield Gap and Yield Constraints 103
6. Farm Size and Income Distribution 116
7. Supply and Demand Elasticities, and Labour Absorption in Rice Cultivation 127
8. Economic Efficiency 142
9. Summary of Major Findings and Policy Implications 150

Appendix 159
Bibliography 169
Index 177

LIST OF TABLES

2.1 Panchayat Unions and Villages in Uthamapalayam Taluk **35**

2.2 Season-wise Average Distribution of Rainfall in Gokilapuram during 1983-84 to 1985-86 **36**

2.3 Area Irrigated by Different Sources in Gokilapuram 1985-86 **38**

2.4 Information on Gokilapuram, 1985-86 **39**

2.5 Caste-wise Classification in Gokilapuram, 1985-86 **40**

2.6 Occupational Classification in Gokilapuram and Uthamapalayam Taluk, 1981 **40**

2.7 Distribution of Operational Land Holding by Size in Gokilapuram, 1985-86 **41**

2.8 Land Utilization Pattern in Gokilapuram, 1985-86 **42**

2.9 Area Under Different Crops in Gokilapuram and Uthamapalayam Taluk, 1985-86 **44**

2.10 Area Under Principal Crops in Gokilapuram, 1985-86 **44**

2.11 Seasons and Varieties of Rice Cultivation in Madurai District **45**

2.12 Variety-wise Rice Cultivation in Gokilapuram, Rabi 1985-86 **46**

2.13 Particulars of Rice Varieties **47**

4.1 Input and Output Structure per acre of IR 20 and CO 37 Rice Varieties, Rabi 1985-86 **88**

4.1.1 Input and Output Structure per acre of IR 20 Farmer Groups, Rabi 1985-86 **89**

4.2 Average Requirements of Hired Labour per acre for Various Farm Activities in Rice Cultivation, Rabi 1985-86 **90**

4.2.1 Average Requirements of Hired Labour per acre for Various Farm Activities by IR 20 Farmer Groups, Rabi 1985-86 **92**

4.3 Cost and Return Structure per acre of IR 20 and CO 37 Varieties of Rice, Rabi 1985-86 **94**

4.3.1 Cost and Return Structure per acre of IR 20 Farmer Groups, Rabi 1985-86 **97**

4.4 Economics of IR 20 and CO 37 Rice Cultivation per acre, Rabi 1985-86 **100**

4.4.1 Economics of IR 20 Rice Cultivation per acre by Farmer Groups, Rabi 1985-86 **101**

5.1 Regression Coefficients for IR 20 Variety of Rice **105**

5.2 Structural Difference between IR 20 Large Farmers and Small Farmers **106**

5.3 Regression Coefficients for CO 37 Variety of Rice **107**

5.4 Structural Difference between IR 20 and CO 37 Varieties of Rice **108**

5.5 Tests of the Stability of Intercept and Slope between IR 20 and CO 37 Varieties of Rice **109**

5.6 Yield Constraints of IR 20 Rice Farmers in Gokilapuram, Rabi 1985-86 **114**

5.7 Yield Constraints of CO 37 Rice Farmers in Gokilapuram, Rabi 1985-86 **114**

6.1 Estimated Regression Equation of the Form: $Y = \beta_0 + \beta_1 X$, IR 20 Rice Variety **117**

6.2 Estimated Regression Equation of the Form: $\log Y = \beta_0 + \beta_1 X$, IR 20 Rice Variety **117**

6.3 Estimated Regression Equation of the Form: $\log Y = \beta_0 + \beta_1 \log X$, IR 20 Rice Variety **118**

6.4 Estimated Regression Equation of the Form: $\log Y = \beta_0 + \beta_1 X$, CO 37 Rice Variety **119**

6.5 Estimated Regression Equation of the Form: $\log Y = \beta_0 + \beta_1 X$, CO 37 Rice Variety **119** ·

6.6 Estimated Regression Equation of the Form: $\log Y = \beta_0 + \beta_1 \log X$, CO 37 Rice Variety **120**

6.7 Distribution of Net Income per acre by Decile Groups of Sample Farmers and Gini Coefficients, Rabi 1985-86 **123**

7.1 Price Variations in the Variables of IR 20 and CO 37 Rice **129**

7.2 Normalised Profit Function and Factor Demand Elasticities for IR 20 and CO 37 Rice Varieties **131**

7.3 Formulae to Estimate Output Supply and Input Demand Elasticities from Cobb-Douglas Profit Function **133**

7.4 Own and Cross Price Elasticities of Demand for Labour and Output Supply for IR 20 and CO 37 Rice Varieties **133**

7.5 Demand for Variable Inputs with respect to its Own Price for IR 20 and CO 37 Rice Varieties **135**

7.6 Own and Cross Price Elasticities of Demand for Variable Inputs for IR 20 and CO 37 Rice Varieties **136**

7.7 Direct and Indirect Estimates of Production Elasticities **138**

8.1 Joint Estimation of Cobb-Douglas Profit Function and Input Demand Equations for IR 20 Rice **146**

8.2 Tests of Economic Efficiency between Small and Large IR 20 Rice Farmers in Gokilapuram, Rabi 1985-86 **147**

LIST OF FIGURES

2.1 Madurai District — Uthamapalayam Taluk **37**

4.1 Operational Cost Structure of IR 20 and CO 37 Varieties of Rice (in percentage) **96**

4.2 Cost and Return Structure of IR 20 and CO 37 Varieties of Rice **99**

5.1 Yield Gap of IR 20 and CO 37 Varieties of Rice **112**

6.1 Farm Size and Productivity **121**

6.2 Lorenz Curves of Net Income Distribution per acre for IR 20 and CO 37 Varieties of Rice in Rabi Season, 1985-86 **124**

1

INTRODUCTION

Plants form 93 per cent of the world's diet. Cereals constitute about two-thirds of all food. Wheat, maize, rice, barley, sorghum, oats, millet and rye are the eight principal cereals which cover 56 per cent of the world's arable land. They constitute the major source of calories and protein for most of the world's people. Wheat (28%), maize (27%) and rice (25%) account for 80 per cent of the global cereal production.[1]

Food crops account for more than 80 per cent of the total cropped area in India. Foodgrains constitute 95.5 per cent of the total area under food crops. Foodgrains comprise 82.6 per cent of cereals and 17.4 per cent of pulses. In the total area under cereals, rice accounts for 36 per cent of the land, followed by wheat (18%), jowar (16%) and bajra (13%) respectively.[2]

Rice occupies a prominent place in Indian agriculture. The area under rice in the country is the largest, accounting for about one-third of the world's area under the crop. Next to China, India ranks second in terms of its production. However, the productivity of about 2.00 tonnes per hectare is very low compared to 4.04 tonnes of Democratic Republic of Korea, 3.79 tonnes of Republic of Korea, 3.73 tonnes of Japan, 2.97 tonnes of Taiwan and 2.86 tonnes of China.[3]

Rice is cultivated in almost all the states of India. The major rice growing States are Punjab, Haryana, Tamil Nadu, Andhra Pradesh, Uttar Pradesh, Jammu and Kashmir, Madhya Pradesh, West Bengal, Orissa, Bihar, Karnataka and Kerala, which together account for 95 per cent of the total rice supply in the country.[4]

1.1 Agricultural Development in India

India had been an exporter of cereals till 1910. Agriculture remained primitive till independence. The partition of India dealt a further blow to the prevailing situation. In the years that followed, cereals came to be imported in large quantities. The population explosion during 1921–1951 brought about a sharp decline in the per capita area cultivated by 20 per cent.[5] The Grow More Food Campaign launched in 1942 had also failed miserably.

Since independence, the Indian government has been emphasising the importance of agricultural development. The sector was given top priority in the First Five Year Plan. The first approach to agricultural development was Extensive Cultivation. The available resources and technology were dispersed over the widest possible area with the hope of producing the fairest possible spread of benefits. It was followed by the Community Development Programme which stressed the integrated development of rural life with increased agricultural production. With the financial assistance from Ford Foundation, 15 Community Development Projects (each covering 100 villages) were started in 1952. Its object was to mobilise rural-dwellers for labour-intensive agricultural productivity projects, supported by certain land reforms, new village cooperatives in which the state would be a partner and national extensive services. However, the land reforms and institutional changes were insufficient to cater to the requirements of the rural mass for intensified cultivation.[6]

In the Second Plan also, agriculture was included in the priority sector. In spite of the numerous efforts made by the government to bridge the gap between demand and supply of foodgrains, attainment of self-sufficiency in food seemed a far cry. So, American experts from the Ford Foundation were invited by the Central Government in the latter half of the Second Five Year Plan to study and recommend measures to improve the agricultural situation in the country through increase in production and productivity. In April 1959, the team submitted a report entitled, "India's Food Crisis and Steps to Meet It". It recommended a selective and intensive approach among farmers and districts, which led to the winding up of the extensive programmes. Based on the report, a new strategy called the Intensive Agricultural District Programme (IADP) was launched in 1960-61. It came to the popularly known as the "Package Programme".[7] Thus, agricultural policies which mainly emphasised institutional reforms and strengthening of agricultural infrastructure in the '50s, shifted their emphasis to increasing land productivity through the use of modern inputs and improved methods of production from 1960-61. Technology came to be recognised as a major input in agricultural production during this period.

The IADP package included better seeds and implements, a balanced dose of fertilizers and pesticides and recommendations about proper soil and water management. It also envisaged a complex of services: technical staff, availability of credit and inputs, land and water improvement, storage, marketing and mechanisms to ensure reliable prices for the cultivators' produce. A new working link was built between research and extension services by setting up a number of agricultural universities supported by the state governments and often given assistance by U.S. educational institutions.[8] Initially, the programme was introduced in the best seven districts of the country, viz., West Godawari (Andhra Pradesh), Shahabad (Bihar), Raipur (Madhya Pradesh), Tanjore (Tamil Nadu), Ludhiana (Punjab), Aligarh (Uttar Pradesh) and Pali (Rajasthan).[9] Due to the considerable progress shown in these districts, eight more districts were brought under the purview of the programme in 1962-63. However, the Fourth Plan draft found that all districts had not achieved the expected progress. Hence in 1964-65, the programme was extended to 114 districts and named Intensive Agricultural Area Programme (IAAP). It aimed at intensive agricultural development of a selected area.

The New Agricultural Strategy (NAS) was initiated in 1966. Under it, policies were formulated to utilise and promote high-yielding varieties of foodgrains in all districts selected under the IADP and IAAP schemes. The NAS was first introduced in the kharif season of 1966. It also came to be known as the High-Yielding Varieties Programme (HYVP).[10]

1.2 High Yielding Varieties Programme (HYVP)

The Green Revolution was an international campaign. It aimed at increasing the productivity of land through scientific technology. The persistent efforts made by the Indian agricultural scientists since the introduction of HYVP resulted in the evolution of numerous high-yielding varieties of principal crops and new farm practices. The main driving force behind the IADP and HYVP was the assumption that agricultural productivity could be increased per acre, given fertile soil, good irrigation facilities with favourable climate and adequate supply of credits and inputs at proper time. Another belief was that given suitable opportunities, the Indian farmers were neither unintelligent nor unduly tradition-bound to favourably respond to the new farm practices.[11]

Under the HYVP, "varietal improvement helps packing into the seed an ability to yield more for a given situation. This potential is best expressed and realised through an appropriate attendant crop management practices more relevant and calls for simultaneously devoting research efforts for its improvement. The crop management practices are closely linked with the land situation and water availability conditions".[12]

On a commercial basis, the planting of seeds from the two international centres of the International Maize and Wheat Improvement Centre (CIMMYT) in Mexico and the International Rice Research Institute (IRRI) in Philippines, first took place in the crop year 1965-66. Within a period of nine years, these seeds covered important proportions of the area planted to wheat and rice in those countries where these crops were of prime importance for food.[13]

With the cooperation of Dr. Norman Borlaug, the first dwarf varieties of wheat introduced in India by the scientists at the Indian Agricultural Research Institute (IARI), New Delhi, in 1962-63. The Central Rice Research Institute at Cuttack and Rice Project Directorate at Hyderabad deal with the development of high-yielding varieties of rice and introduction of new farm practices. Ever since, a number of rice research centres have been established in India to deal with problems specific to a region or state. At present, there are as many as 120 rice research stations in the country. Currently, the IARI is paying attention to the improvement of the nutritional quality of major foodgrains such as wheat, rice, millet, maize, sorghum, and so on.[14]

The HYVP has been carried out to a great extent by the individual state's agricultural and administrative authorities. Initially, the HYVP (1966-67) was implemented in a total area of 1.89 million hectares. This increased to 9.2 million hectares on the eve of the Fourth Five Year Plan. The Fifth Plan stressed on agricultural and rural development. In 1984-85, the total area under HYVP remarkably increased to 55.42 million hectares, which accounted for 31.6 per cent of the gross cropped area.[15]

The implementation of HYVP has brought about an increase in rice production. The area under rice increased from 30 million hectares in 1950-51 to 41 million hectares in 1984-85. The corresponding rise in production were 20 million tonnes and 59 million tonnes respectively. There has been a tremendous increase in yield from 668 kg. per hectare to 1425 kg. per hectare over the period.[16] This increase was the result of the expansion in supplies of inputs and extension services to farmers and better farm management. The distribution of seeds, fertilizers, pesticides and insecticides and institutional credits shows marked increase over the years.

1.3 Agricultural Price Policy

Food is one of the basic necessities of human life. Economic stability of a country largely depends on foodgrain prices. More attention is paid to the prices of foodgrains because they enter the consumption basket directly and any short supply in food would seriously affect the mass. Demand for foodgrains being price inelastic, even the slightest shortage in output supply tends to cause a substantial rise in its prices.

Owing to the growing population, increased urbanisation and rising per capita income, the increase in demand for foodgrains was greater than the increase in supplies of foodgrains produced under the constraints of inadequate irrigation facilities, insufficient input supply and weak market infrastructure. As a result, the supply of foodgrains fell short of its output in the country. The first step to evolving an agricultural price policy was the formation of Foodgrains Policy Committee in 1947. The Committee recommended a policy of progressive decontrol, reduction of dependence on imports of foodgrains in orderly and planned stages and substantial increase of domestic production as early as possible. The Foodgrains Procurement Committee appointed in 1950 recommended the continuation and extension of the system of rationing and controlled distribution.

Due to the easy situation on food front in the early years of First Five Year Plan, the government policy shifted from complete control to complete decontrol. However, due to rising trend in foodgrain prices in the mid-'50s, the government had to reintroduce partial controls. A Foodgrains Enquiry Committee was set up in 1957 to stabilise prices. The Committee recommended building up of buffer stocks, disposal of surplus stocks to deficit states, licensing wholesale traders and fixation of minimum and maximum prices.

Till early 1960s, the main thrust of food price policy was to ensure that shortages in food supply did not cause excessive rise in consumer prices. Any such shortages were immediately compensated through imports to protect the interests of consumers. The imports helped in containing the price by curbing undue price increases. Consequently, the farmers did not receive any significant support from the government. The public distribution out of imports and zonal restrictions further depressed the prices. As a result, production of foodgrains showed no significant uptrend.

One of the major uncertainties affecting farming activity is a sudden fall in prices. Hence, the focus of food policy in Third Five Year Plan was shifted to ensuring incentive prices to the farmers. A Foodgrains Prices Committee was appointed in 1964 to recommend 'fair and economic prices'. A policy of fixing support prices for cereals was adopted in this year. In January 1965, Agricultural Price Commission was set up to advise the government on evolving an integrated price structure to increase production and also to protect the consumers. Another Foodgrains Policy Committee was appointed in 1966 to give recommendations on minimum, procurement and issue prices. Its important recommendations were: (i) announcement of guaranteed minimum support prices in advance of the sowing season as an incentive for increasing production; and (ii) procurement price to be fixed higher than support price, based on proper incentive to the producers and reasonable price for the consumers. The Food Corporation of India (FCI) was set up in 1965 for the procurement, storage and distribution of foodgrains. The food policy assured the farmers that their incomes would not be affected by any shortages in demand or excess supply of output.

The evolution of New Agricultural Strategy coincided with the effective implementation of agricultural price policy. The Fourth Plan acknowledged the importance of the policy of minimum support prices as an incentive to agricultural production and the role of FCI, State Trading Corporation and Cooperative Marketing Organisations in making it effective. The Fifth and Sixth Plans accepted the price policy as being of crucial importance in agricultural development. The Seventh Plan felt that the support prices of rice and wheat, backed by arrangement for procurement, had contributed to the reduction of fluctuations, maintenance of profitability and stimulation of steady growth. It also recommended the determination of appropriate relative prices for different crops with a view to ensuring efficient use of resources.[17]

Despite the existence of Food Corporation of India and the support prices provided by other state agencies, the rice support price policy was not adequately effective. The main break-through in rice production came in the mid-'60s with the cultivation of IR varieties on a commercial basis. It was adequately supported by a remunerative price support policy. The rice price rose by 30 to 40 per cent in 1973-74 and further by 37 per cent in 1977-78 to 1980-81. This provided the necessary boost to rice cultivation both in area covered and output produced.[18]

1.4 Agriculture in Tamil Nadu

Agriculture is the primary sector of Tamil Nadu (TN). It is the most important single source of the state's income and employment. It forms a strong and prosperous base of the state's economic growth. As at the all India level, foodgrains dominate the agricultural economy of Tamil Nadu. Paddy has been the most important food crop, accounting for 54 per cent of its total area in the state. The yield of 2.5 tonnes per hectare of rice is among the highest in India. Tamil Nadu heads all other states in the number of pumpsets energised in the country.[19] The state accounts for 7.46 per cent of the total area under paddy but contributes 13.75 per cent of the total rice production in the country.[20]

At the district level, foodgrains continue to dominate the economy of nine districts (Chengalpattu, Dharmapuri, Madurai, South Arcot, Ramanathapuram, Coimbatore, Tiruchirappalli, Thanjavur and Pudukottai) with more than 60 per cent of their gross cropped area under foodgrains. The proportion of acreage under paddy has decreased in most of the districts, while it has been increasing in Chengalpattu, Madurai, Tirunelveli, Salem and Ramanathapuram, due to the increase in irrigated area in them.[21]

The impressive expansion in rice production during the 1950s in the state was brought about by an expansion in the area under the crop rather than increase in yield. The increase in rice production from 19.3 lakh tonnes in 1950-51 to 35.6 lakh tonnes in 1960-61 was due to the increase in area under its cultivation. The introduction of High-Yielding Varieties Programme in the mid-'60s, brought about a significant increase in the production and productivity of foodgrains in the state. The locally improved varieties of rice like ADT-27 and

CO-29 were less responsive to fertilizer and liable to lodge. On the other hand, varieties like IR 5, IR 8, IR 20 and IR 22, introduced from 1966-67, were more fertilizer-responsive.[22]

The yield and production of rice which were only 1050 kg. per hectare and 33.3 lakh tonnes in 1959-60, respectively rose to the level of 1899 kg. per hectare and 46.2 lakh tonnes in 1970-71. The yield exceeded 2.0 tonnes per hectare in 1978-79 and the production increased to 55.6 lakh tonnes. This phenomenal increase in the productivity and production of rice has been termed "Rice Revolution". While 'wheat revolution' is the pride of Punjab, Tamil Nadu can claim to be going through a 'rice revolution'.[23]

The compound growth rate of production which was 1.6 per cent per annum in the decade preceding the seed-fertilizer technology (i.e., 1955-56 to 1965-66) increased to 3.3 per cent per annum, following the introduction of High-Yielding Varieties Programme (i.e., 1966-67 to 1979-80). This rise in the growth rate and output of rice is attributed to the wide-spread cultivation of high-yielding varieties, expansion of irrigation facilities, increased use of fertilizer, higher profitability and changes in the cropping pattern in favour of rice.[24]

The focus of Tamil Nadu government's strategy on increasing the productivity of rice is evident from: (i) the implementation of Operation 5 M.T. of paddy per hectare through 'lab to the farm' technology; (ii) assignment of an important place to IR varieties; and (iii) the importance given to certified seed production and distribution.

Since 1983-84, there is a steady increase in the production and area covered by rice in the state. During 1981-82, the yield per hectare of rice rose to 2,265 kg. in Tamil Nadu. The average yield of 2,372 kg. per hectare in 1985-86 has been an all-time highest realisation in rice production. At present, Tamil Nadu ranks third in the country, next to Punjab (3,199 kg/ha) and Haryana (2,797 kg/ha) in terms of average rice yield. Today, Tamil Nadu is not only self-sufficient in rice production but is also able to export it to other deficit states in the country.

Since the early 1980s, the area under high-yielding varieties of paddy in particular has gained momentum. There has been a remarkable increase in the coverage of area by high-yielding varieties since the initiation of the programme in 1966-67. The area under high-yielding varieties of rice has increased from seven per cent to the total cropped area under the crop in 1966-67 to 96.5 per cent in 1985-86. Among the high-yielding varieties rice, IR varieties stand out to be the most popular over the years among rice farmers. It accounted for 86 per cent of the total area under HYV paddy in 1985-86.[25]

1.5 Statement of the Problem

Agriculture is beset with several problems. It would be over-ambitious to try to deal with all of them in the present study. Hence, only some of the main problems in the sector, especially the production aspects, have been discussed with respect to rice cultivation in Gokilapuram village. They are cost and returns, determinants of yield, yield gap and yield constraints, farm size and productivity, inequalities in the distribution of farm income from rice cultivation, labour absorption, output supply and input demand elasticities in response to changes in prices and economic efficiency of farmer groups.

The encouraging results of the introduction of HYVP in agriculture is of fundamental importance in India's quest for increasing food production. The relative importance of rice crop in the country and state justifies its selection for analysis. In view of the considerable number of Exotic Varieties (EV) and Location-Specific Varieties (LSV) released and the large acreages reportedly planted with them, it is imperative to make a comparative study of two such popular varieties (IR 20 and CO 37) in the selected village.

Since the introduction of the New Agricultural Strategy (NAS) in 1965, rice cultivation in India has traversed a long way. It has had varying impact on different crops and its varieties, in different areas and also on different classes of farmers within the same area. With the wide-spread use of high-yielding varieties and modern technology, input use has also been increasing with the rising yields. This calls for a comparative study of the levels of input application and the monetary and physical returns accruing to each rice variety and to large and small farmer groups operating in the study area.

The Green Revolution which heralded the transition of agriculture from the traditional to a modern stage, promised increased agricultural output. Since the determination of yield is affected by cultivation techniques, an understanding of the contribution of each input to the growth of output of the two varieties is of vital importance. The different natural and physical resource endowments, efficiency, prices, constraints and pace and levels of adoption of the technology would lead to the choice of different factor proportions. This warrants a similar analysis of yield determinants for the small and large farmers in Gokilapuram.

It is reported that the rice yield achieved under field conditions has generally failed to approach their experimental yield potential (Swaminathan,[26] Davidson and Martin,[27] Mukherji[28] and Kalirajan[29]). A further gap exists between the maximum yield attained at farm and the average yield realised by the farmers in the same region (Flinn and Ali[30]). The factors preventing farmers from achieving the full potential of the technology could be bio-physical, economic or social in nature. This necessitates an analysis of the magnitude of yield gap that exists between the maximum and average yield in the case of each variety in the study area. It is also important to identify the socio-economic factors that restrict farmers from achieving the potential yield at farm level.

There has been a significant divergence of views relating to the relationship between farm size and farm efficiency. Some of the earlier studies have reported the existence of an inverse relationship in Indian agriculture (Hanumantha Rao,[31] Sen[32] and Khusro[33]), while other studies indicate the weakening or even the disappearance of the inverse relationship (Rudra and Sen,[34] Ghosh,[35] Hanumantha Rao,[36] Usha[37] and Saini[38]). However, no definite conclusion has been so far reached on the issue. Hence, a probe into the nature of relationship between farm size and farm efficiency in the study area becomes indispensable.

One of the outcomes of the New Agricultural Strategy has been inequalities in farm incomes. It is strongly believed that the benefits of the new strategy have not been shared equally by farmers within and between varieties and regions due to the differential adoption rate and factor endowments (Kalirajan and Shand,[39] Raj,[40] Byres[41] and Kalirajan[42]). Therefore, it is important to understand the impact of the cultivation of the two rice varieties on the income distribution of its growers in the village.

One of the main objectives of agricultural policy is to increase output. An appropriate price policy with respect to factor inputs and output is essential to encourage the adoption of the modern technology. Hence, it is necessary to analyse the responsiveness of farmers to changes in the prices of factor inputs and rice. Further, the high-yielding varieties promise to raise the employment potentials radically through multiple cropping pattern, high level usage of modern inputs, etc. (Sharma,[43] Bisaliah,[44] Kalirajan and Shand[45] and Johl[46]). Therefore, it is also important to study the labour absorption capacity of the two varieties in response to changes in rice price and the prices of inputs.

Another debated issue in agriculture is the economic efficiency of farmer groups. Given the resources at their command and the knowledge of production possibilities — resources use and allocation efficiency of farmers working in the same atmosphere may tend to differ. The studies of Hanumantha Rao[47] and Khan and Maki[48] reported large farmers to be economically more efficient, while Lau and Yotopoulos[49] found small farmers to be more efficient and still others (Kalirajan,[50] Rajagopalan[51] and Parthasarthy and Prasad[52]) observed both the farmer groups to be equally efficient. A similar investigation into the efficiency behaviour of small and large farmer groups in Gokilapuram assumes great importance in the study.

1.6 Objectives and Methodology

The main objectives pursued in the study are as follows:

1. To study the cost and return structure of IR 20 and CO 37 rice varieties and of small and large farmer groups cultivating IR 20 rice.
2. To identify the main determinants of yield and factors causing yield gap with regard to the two varieties.
3. To examine the relationship between farm size and farm efficiency with respect to IR 20 and CO 37 rice.
4. To study the inequalities in net income distribution from the cultivation of the two varieties.
5. To investigate the labour absorption capacity of each rice variety and to study the supply responsiveness of the two varieties with regard to their own prices and the prices of variable inputs and units of fixed inputs. Further, the study also makes an attempt to examine the validity of Mellor's[53] hypothesis that output prices have no effect on their supply.
6. To analyse the economic efficiency of the IR 20 farmer groups.

The cost structure was analysed by classifying it into cost A and cost C. The returns were estimated in terms of both physical and monetary units.

Multiple regression model was used to identify the major determinants of yield. Yield gap was estimated as the difference between maximum yield and average yield realised by farmers in the study area. Garrett's ranking technique was used to rank the major constraints to potential yield at farm.

Simple linear regressions were employed to study the relationship between farm size and farm efficiency. Inequalities in income distribution was examined using Gini coefficient.

Cobb-Douglas profit function was estimated along with four input demand functions to study the labour absorption, supply responsiveness and input demand and economic efficiency of farmers. It was jointly estimated using Zellner's seemingly unrelated regression which provides asymptotically more efficient estimates.

1.7 Scope of the Study

Agricultural sector occupies a strategic position in India. It contributes directly towards the economic growth of the country. It provides employment to 68.7 per cent of the total work force. It contributes 38.3 per cent of the net domestic product and more than one-third of the net domestic income. It plays an important role in industrial development by providing the necessary raw materials and market for industrial products. It caters to about 60 per cent of the requirements of the society. The share of agriculture and industries based on it has been around 70 to 75 per cent in the total export earnings. Thus agricultural development has a significant impact on the overall economic development of the country. Obviously, it is also one of the most important instruments to achieve a break-through in the rural setting, as it exerts an important influence on the socio-economic life of the people.[54] Hence a detailed study on the various aspects of agrarian sector assumes great importance in framing appropriate policies for its development.

Rice is an important food crop in India. It is the primary food of the largest section of people. As fluctuations in rice production would affect the consumers in particular and national balance of trade at large, there is a need for policies which would increase rice production and incomes of farmers on one hand and avoid food deficiency in the country on the other. To combat food problems prevailing in the country, the High-Yielding Varieties Programme was introduced. The present study endeavours to examine the feasibility of cultivation of two popular high-yielding rice varieties at village level.

The study is basically a micro level study. A micro study helps to understand problems specific to a particular region and to provide relevant solutions in its proper perspective. Further, the evaluation of performance of crops in a homogeneous state would provide better judgements on them. Micro-economic policies may be used as a guiding factor in pursuing macro-economic policies. In fact, it would be more appropriate to formulate macro-economic objectives of development based on micro-economic experiences. Keeping these ideas in view, the study is focussed on Gokilapuram village in Uthamapalayam taluk of Madurai district, Tamil Nadu. The findings at the village level would be useful in the formulation of economic policies relevant to its problems.

Cost of cultivation plays an important role in the determination of price. A study on the cost and return structure of IR 20 and CO 37 rice varieties would provide an insight into their economic and physical performances. This would help rice growers to select the variety more suitable and profitable for cultivation.

An analysis of rice cultivation using the criterion of size of farm would highlight the pattern of cost and return structure of large and small farmers. This would help in the formulation of policies on land reforms and suggestions on institutional aids.

A study on the determinants of yield would be useful in examining the degree of influence exercised by each factor of production on yield. This would help in suggesting possible ways of improving farm management. An analysis of yield gap would contribute to an understanding of the extent of gap that exists between maximum yield and average yield at farm level in the study area. An identification of the causes of yield gap under farmers' conditions would help in locating the factors responsible for it. This would be useful in suggesting measures to bridge the yield gap by overcoming the constraints and thus achieving the potential yield at farm level and enjoy the full benefits of rice cultivation.

An analysis of the relationship between farm size and productivity would provide important information on the nature of relationship that prevails between them in the village. It would provide an important policy implications on land reforms and land ceilings on holdings. An examination of the inequalities in income distribution of the two varieties would help in understanding the pattern of net income distribution among farmers.

Price policy is one of the principal tools that the government possesses to influence the allocation of inputs, increase production and income, etc. A study on the supply responsiveness of each rice variety to changes in its own price and the prices of variable inputs and units of fixed inputs would aid the formulation of suitable policies to increase rice output. Further, in the context of mounting unemployment and disguised unemployment in the agricultural sector, a study on the labour absorptive capacity in response to changes in the prices of output and factor inputs would be important in evaluating the employment potentialities of the two varieties.

Economic efficiency is an indicator of the farmers' efficacy in converting given inputs into output. An analysis of economic efficiency of large and small farmer groups in the study area would provide information on their relative efficiency. The identification of technical and price efficiency would provide better predictions and implications on land consolidation policy.

Thus the study as a whole would help in the formulation of suitable policies with regard to the problems of the village in particular and regions with similar situations in general.

1.8 Limitations of the Study

This is a micro level study confined to a particular village. Differences in natural and physical resources, agrarian structure, irrigation sources, cropping pattern, varieties of crops cultivated, the pace and level of adoption of the new technology, etc., contribute to inter- and intra-regional disparities in the gains realised by the farming community. Hence the findings of th- study cannot be generalised, as it is restricted to Gokilapuram village.

Agricultural performance in each year largely depends on the monsoon which may give high profits in one year and unexpected losses in another. The findings of this study are based on data limited to rabi season of the agricultural year 1985-86. Kharif season was not taken into account as IR 20 and CO 37 cultivation are not popular during the season in the village.

Further, the analysis confines itself to two popular varieties of rice in the village. Therefore, the findings cannot be generalised for the crop as a whole.

The limited number of farmers cultivating CO 37 rice did not make it possible to classify them into small and large farmer groups. So they were studied in toto, unlike in the case of IR 20 rice where such a classification was made and studied separately.

The varied conditions in India requires different policy-mix for each region. Nevertheless, although there are obvious limitations to this study, they are not so strong as to invalidate its findings. Rather than trying to be exhaustive, the study only aims at providing a balanced account of the existing state in the agricultural sector of Gokilapuram village during the rabi season of 1985-86. It would provide a picture of what might occur in regions with similar conditions.

1.9 Chapter Scheme

Following the introductory chapter, Chapter 2 provides a glimpse of some of the geographical, social and economic characteristics of the study area. It further provides a description of the sample design, variables used and their measurements.

The different concepts used in the study are explained in Chapter 3. It also provides a brief review of some of the related literature on the study.

In Chapter 4 the cost and return structure of the two rice varieties and of large and small farmer groups cultivating IR 20 rice is discussed in detail.

An attempt is made towards the identification of the important determinants of yield of the two varieties and of IR 20 farmer groups in Chapter 5. An analysis of yield gap and its constraints with respect to the two varieties is also done in it.

The relationship between farm size and productivity is examined for the two varieties in Chapter 6. It also explores the inequalities in income distribution arising out of the cultivation of the two rice varieties.

Chapter 7 makes a study on the supply elasticity of each variety to changes in their own prices and to the prices of variable inputs and units of fixed inputs. It further analyses the labour absorption capacity of each variety in response to changes in output price and prices of inputs.

An attempt is made in Chapter 8 to examine the relative economic efficiency of small and large farmer groups producing IR 20 rice.

The major findings of the study and its policy implications are summarised in the final chapter.

NOTES

1. R.W. Stubb and Others, "Introduction", *Cereal Disease Methodology Manual*, CIMMYT, Mexico, 1986, p. 1.
2. "Food Front Bright", *Manorama Year Book*, (Ed.) K.M. Mathew, Manorama Publishing House, Kerala, 1987, pp. 562-567.
3. R.K. Mahajan, A.V. Rao and D. Gandhi, "Rice Production in India During 1970s", *Agricultural Situation in India*, Vol. XL, No. 11, February, 1986, p. 987.
4. H.K. Pande and K. Srinivasa Rao, "Rice Rescarch in India — Recent Advances", *Advances in Indian Agriculture*, (Ed.) S.P. Rayachaudhuri, Vol. 1, Books and Periodicals Agency, New Delhi, 1983, p. 37.
5. D.V. Raghava Rao, "Modern Farm Technology: Sociological Aspects", *New Seeds: Adoption and Yield*, J.P. Singh, et. al., Sterling Publishers Pvt. Ltd., New Delhi, 1979, p. 279.
6. Andrew Pearse, "Promotion of the New Technology", *Seeds of Plenty, Seeds of Want — Social and Economic Implications of the Green Revolution*, Clarendon Press, Oxford, 1980, p. 80.
7. Raghava Rao, loc.cit.
8. D.K. Desai, "Intensive Agricultural District Programme", *Economic and Political Weekly*, Review of Agriculture, Vol. IV, No. 2, June 1969, pp. A-83—A-90.
9. S.K. Misra and V.K. Puri, "Agricultural Inputs and Green Revolution", *Indian Economy*, Himalaya Publishing House, Delhi, 1986, p. 432.
10. A.N. Sadhu and R.K. Mahajan, "Technological Change and Agricultural Growth in India", *Technological Change and Agricultural Development in India*, Himalaya Publishing House, Delhi, 1985, pp. 3-9.
11. Raghava Rao, op.cit., pp. 279-280.
12. Pande and Srinivasa Rao, op.cit., p. 42.
13. Pearse, "Political Motors of Technological Innovations", op.cit., p. 37.
14. S.P. Rayachaudhuri, "Development of Agriculture in India Since 2500 B.C.", (Ed.) Rayachaudhuri, op.cit., p. 26.
15. Misra and Puri, loc.cit.
16. Mahajan, Rao and Gandhi, loc.cit.
17. Misra and Puri, "Agricultural Prices and Agricultural Price Policy", op.cit., pp. 537-555.
18. A.S. Kahlon and D.S. Tyagi, "Evolution of Agricultural Price Policy", *Agricultural Price Policy in India*, Allied Publishers Pvt. Ltd., New Delhi, 1983, pp. 276-406.
19. R.N. Poduval, "Adoption of New Technology", *Foodgrain Economy of Tamil Nadu: Problems and Prospects*, Emerald Publishers, Madras, 1987, p. 35.

20. C. Arputharaj, *Agricultural Development Potential in Tamil Nadu*, Lecture delivered at the Department of Economics, Madurai Kamaraj University, Madurai, 26th February 1983, p. 12.
21. Poduval, "Changes in the Cropping Pattern within Foodgrains", op.cit., pp. 17-18,
22. *Ibid.*, "Adoption of New Technology", p. 32.
23. *Ibid.*, p. 33.
24. *Ibid.*, p. 37.
25. "Agriculture and Allied Activities", *Tamil Nadu — An Economic Appraisal: 1985-86*, Evaluation and Applied Research Department, Madras, 1987, pp. 13-38.
26. M.S. Swaminathan, Lecture, *The Hindu*, 19th March 1983, in "Bridging Gap in Yields between Average Farms and Research Centres", *Monthly Reporter*, Vol. 9, No. 5, Director of Agriculture, Madras, October 1983, pp. 1-6.
27. B.R. Davidson and B.R. Martin, "The Relationship between Yields on Farms and in Experiments", *Australian Journal of Agricultural Economics*, Vol. 9, No. 2, December 1965, pp. 129-140.
28. D.K. Mukherji, *Gap Analysis: An Effective Production Increase Concept in Rice*, Summary of Lecture delivered at the State Level Training Meeting on Rice held at Purila, Department of Agriculture, West Bengal, India, July 1977.
29. K. Kalirajan, "The Contribution of Location Specific Research to Agricultural Productivity", *Indian Journal of Agricultural Economics*, Vol. 35, No. 4, October-December 1980, pp. 8-16.
30. J.C. Flinn and Mubarak Ali, "Technical Efficiency in Basmati Rice Production", *Pakistan Journal of Applied Economics*, Vol. 5, No. 1, 1986, pp. 1-22.
31. C.H. Hanumantha Rao, "Alternative Explanation of the Inverse Relationship between Farm Size and Output Per Acre in India", *Indian Economic Review*, (New Series), Vol. 1, No. 2, October 1966, pp. 1-12.
32. A.K. Sen, "Size of Holding and Productivity", *Economic and Political Weekly*, Annual No., Vol. XVI, Nos. 5, 6 & 7, February 1964.
33. A.M. Khusro, "Returns to Scale in Indian Agriculture", *Indian Journal of Agricultural Economics*, Vol. XIX, Nos. 3 & 4, July-December 1964, pp. 51-80.
34. Ashok Rudra and A.K. Sen, "Farm Size and Labour Use: Analysis and Policy", *Economic and Political Weekly*, Annual No., Vol. XV, Nos. 5, 6 & 7, February 1980, pp. 391-394.
35. Madhusudan Ghosh, "Farm Size Productivity Nexus under Alternative Technology", *Indian Journal of Agricultural Economics*, Vol. 41, No. 1, January-March 1986, pp. 17-28.
36. C.H. Hanumantha Rao, "Farm Size and the Distribution of Gain", *Technological Change and Distribution of Gains in Indian Agriculture*, Macmillan Company of India Ltd., Delhi, 1975, pp. 136-150.
37. Usha Rani, "Size of Farm and Productivity", *Economic and Political Weekly*, Vol. VI, No. 26, June 26, 1971, pp. A-85—A-89.
38. G.R. Saini, "Holding Size, Productivity and Some Related Aspects of Indian Agriculture", *Economic and Political Weekly*, Vol. VI, No. 26, June 26, 1971, pp. A-71—A-85.
39. K. Kalirajan and R.T. Shand, "Location Specific Research: Rice Technology in India", *Land Economics*, Vol. 58, No. 4, November 1982, pp. 537-546.

40. K.N. Raj, "Some Questions Concerning Growth: Transformation and Planning of Agriculture in Developing Countries", *Journal of Development Planning*, Vol. 1, No. 1, 1969, pp. 15-38.
41. T. Byres, "Dialectics of Green Revolution", *South Asia Review*, Vol. 5, No. 2, 1972, pp. 99-116.
42. K. Kalirajan, "Benefits from the High-Yielding Varieties Programme and their Distribution in an Irrigated Paddy Area", *Indian Journal of Agricultural Economics*, Vol. 35, No. 3, July-September 1980, pp. 70-76.
43. R.K. Sharma, "Green Revolution and Farm Employment: An Analysis of Experience in Punjab", *Indian Journal of Industrial Relations*, Vol. 10, No. 2, October 1974.
44. S. Bisaliah, "Decomposition Analysis of Employment Change under New Production Technology in Punjab Agriculture", *Indian Journal of Agricultural Economics*, Vol. 33, No. 2, April-June 1978, pp. 70-80.
45. K. Kalirajan and R.T. Shand, "Labour Absorption in Tamil Nadu Agriculture: A Micro Analysis", *Journal of Developing Economies*, Vol. XX, No. 3, September 1981, pp. 333-343.
46. S.S. Johl, *Mechanization, Labour Use and Productivity in Indian Agriculture*, Ohio State University, 1974.
47. Hanumantha Rao, loc.cit.
48. Mahmood H. Khan and Dennis R. Maki, "Effects of Farm Size on Economic Efficiency: The Case of Pakistan", *American Journal of Agricultural Economics*, Vol. 61, February 1979, pp. 64-69.
49. L.J. Lau and P.A. Yotopoulos, "A Test for Relative Efficiency and Application to Indian Agriculture", *American Economic Review*, Vol. 61, March 1971, pp. 94-109.
50. K. Kalirajan, "The Economic Efficiency of Farmers Growing High-Yielding, Irrigated Rice in India", *American Journal of Agricultural Economics*, Vol. 63, No. 3, August 1981, pp. 566-570.
51. V. Rajagopalan, "North Arcot, Tamil Nadu", *Changes in Rice Farming in Selected Areas of Asia*, International Rice Research Institute, Philippines, 1975, pp. 71-91.
52. G. Parthasarthy and D.S. Prasad, "Response to the Impact of the New Rice Technology by Farm Size and Tenure: Andhra Pradesh", Interpretive Analysis of Selected Papers from *Changes in Rice Farming in Selected Areas in Asia*, International Rice Research Institute, Philippines, 1978, pp. 111-127.
53. J.W. Mellor, "Determinants of Rural Poverty: The Dynamics of Production, Technology and Prices", *Agricultural Change and Rural Poverty*, (Eds.) J.W. Mellor and G.M. Desai, Food Policy Research Institute, Washington, D.C., 1985, pp. 21-40.
54. Misra and Puri, "Indian Agriculture: Role, Nature and Cropping Pattern", op.cit., pp. 401-403.

2

GOKILAPURAM: ITS PROFILE, SAMPLE DESIGN AND MEASUREMENT OF VARIABLES

The chapter presents a brief description of Gokilapuram — the area selected for the study. Based on primary and secondary data, it provides an insight into the human and physical resources of the village. Further, it highlights some of the main features of its socio-economic structure. It also explains the sample design adopted and the measurement of important variables used in the study.

2.1 Gokilapuram

Madurai is one among the 20 districts of Tamil Nadu, with agriculture as its dominant sector. The district was selected due to the relatively higher productivity of rice in it in the state. Besides, the area under irrigation and adoption of modern technology in rice cultivation is also comparatively greater in it.[1] This induced the researcher to select Madurai district for the purpose of the study.

The district consists of 13 taluks, of which Uthamapalayam is one of the most promising and progressive taluks in rice cultivation. It consists of four Panchayat Unions, comprising 54 villages. They are as follows[2]:–

TABLE 2.1: Panchayat Unions and Villages in Uthamapalayam Taluk

	Panchayat Unions	Number of Villages Covered
(i)	Uthamapalayam	11
(ii)	Bodinayakanur	15
(iii)	Chinnamanur	17
(iv)	Cumbum Valley	11
	Total Villages	54

Gokilapuram is one of the 54 villages belonging to Uthamapalayam firka of Uthamapalayam taluk in Madurai district. It is located in the more prosperous and relatively advanced agrarian region of Cumbum valley. Uthamapalayam taluk lies between latitudes 9°34 and 10°10 North and longitudes 77°10 and 77°28 East. Gokilapuram is about six kms. East of the taluk centre.[3] The location of Gokilapuram village in Uthamapalayam taluk is shown in Fig. 2.1.

Soil

Gokilapuram is gifted with rich soil for agricultural cultivation. The type of soil in the region is sandy loam to red loam with low nitrogen, medium phosphorous and high potassium content. This soil is suited for rice cultivation.

Rainfall

The rainfall recording station for Gokilapuram is located at Uthamapalayam taluk. Table 2.2 presents the season-wise average rainfall in the village during the agricultural years 1983-84 to 1985-86.

TABLE 2.2: Season-wise Average Distribution of Rainfall in Gokilapuram during 1983-84 to 1985-86

Season	Months	Average Annual Rainfall in mm	Number of Rainy Days	Percentage to Average Annual Rainfall
1. South West Monsoon	June-September	235.83	32	31.52
2. North East Monsoon	October-December	247.03	21	33.02
3. Winter	January-February	68.20	7	9.12
4. Summer	March-May	197.10	13	26.34
Total		748.16	73	100

Source: Weather Report, Taluk Office, Uthamapalayam, 1983-86.

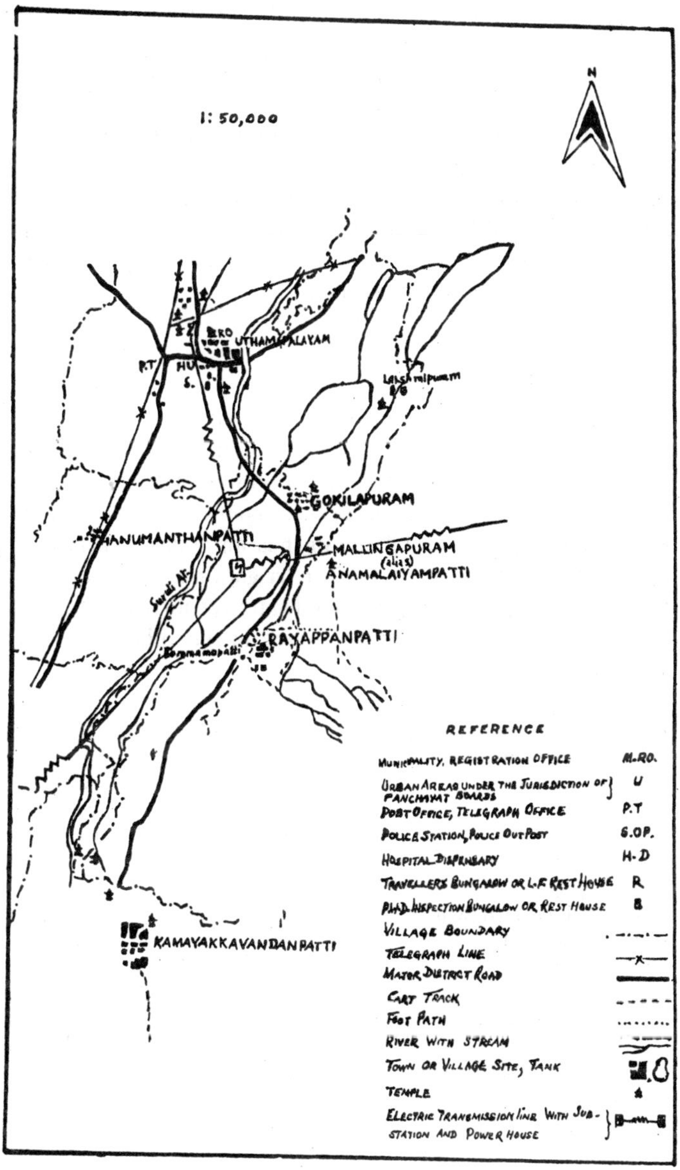

FIG. 2.1: Madurai District — Uthamapalayam Taluk

The village had sufficient rains over the years. The highest rainfall was received in the North East monsoon (247.03 mm) for 21 days. In the South West monsoon period, the region experienced rains upto 235.83 mm over 32 days. In winter, the rains were the lowest (9.12 mm). There were 13 rainy days in summer, ranging upto 197.10 mm.

Thus, the heaviest rainfall was recorded during the North East monsoon, accounting for 33.02 per cent of the total rainfall during the period. About 31.52 per cent of the rains was received during the South West monsoon. Rains during summer was 26.34 per cent, while in winter it was quite scanty.

2.2 Irrigation

Backed by active credit institutions and good extension services, the existence of a reliable irrigation system is the most important infrastructure necessary for the adoption of the new agricultural technology. It acts as an insurance against uncertain rainfalls and hence reduces risk. Gokilapuram has an assured surface irrigation facility. It is served by the Periyar Irrigation System round the year. In addition, it also has good groundwater resources.

The extent of irrigation by source in the village is illustrated by Table 2.3.

TABLE 2.3: Area Irrigated by Different Sources in Gokilapuram, 1985-86

	Particulars	Number	Area in Acres	Percentage to Total Area Irrigated
Total Cropped Area			1525.03	
1.	Net Area Irrigated		768.45	
2.	Irrigation by:			
	(i) Well	14	17.00	1.14
	(ii) Tank	1	98.00	6.55
	(iii) Canal	1	1380.17	92.30
3.	Total Area Irrigated		1495.17	100

Source: Adangal, Village Account No.2, Fasli Year 1395, Gokilapuram, 1985-86.

In Gokilapuram, 1525.03 acres of land was cultivated during 1985-86. Of it, as much as 1495.17 acres were irrigated by well, tank and canal sources. In other words, 98.04 per cent of the total area sown was irrigated in the village.

Canal system was the primary source, covering 92.30 per cent of the total irrigated area. Tank irrigated about seven per cent of it. Well constituted a very small component of the total irrigation. The extent of net area irrigated in the village was 768.45 acres during the year.

2.3 **General Information**

The general information on the study area are given in Table 2.4.

TABLE 2.4: Information on Gokilapuram, 1985-86

Particulars	Gokilapuram
1. Total Geographical Area in Acres	1034.73
2. Size of Population (1981 Census)	4201
(a) Male	2049
(b) Female	2152
(i) Cultivators	803
(ii) Agricultural labourers	1027
3. Number of Households	926
4. Average Size of Family	5
5. Total Cropped Area in Acres	1525.03
6. Area under Rice in Acres	1439.46

Source: Adangal, Gokilapuram, 1985-86.

There were 926 households in the village during 1985-86. The 1981 Census recorded its total population to be 4201 persons (2049 male and 2152 female). The average size of family in the village was five. Of the total working force, 803 were cultivators and 1027 agricultural labourers.

Gokilapuram spreads over an area of 1034.73 acres. The total cropped area in the village was 1525.03 acres, of which, 1439.46 acres (94.39%) were under rice cultivation in 1985-86. This indicates the prominence of cultivation in the village.

Caste-wise Classification

Table 2.5 depicts the major caste-wise classification of households in Gokilapuram.

TABLE 2.5: Caste-wise Classification in Gokilapuram, 1985-86

	Main Caste	Number of Households	Percentage of Total Households
1.	Forward Castes	–	–
2.	Backward Castes	635	67
3.	Scheduled Castes	301	33
4.	Scheduled Tribes	–	–
	Total	926	100

Source: Adangal, Gokilapuram, 1985-86.

Of the 926 households in the village, 67 per cent belonged to backward class and the rest to Scheduled Castes. It was surprising to note that there were no households belonging to forward castes or Scheduled Tribes in the village. This information was verified not only with the village officials, but also with a cross-section of the people in Gokilapuram.

Occupational Classification

Table 2.6 reports details on the occupational classification of the work force in Gokilapuram and Uthamapalayam taluk, according to the 1981 Census.

TABLE 2.6: Occupational Classification in Gokilapuram and Uthamapalayam Taluk, 1981

	Occupation	Percentage of Total Workers	
		Gokilapuram	Uthamapalayam Taluk
1.	Cultivators	20.04	18.32
2.	Agricultural labourers	59.97	57.30
3.	Others (Mining, Manufacturing, Construction, Trade, Commerce and Other Services)	19.99	24.38
	Total	100.00	100.00

Source: 1981 Census and Madhura, "The Setting: Gokilapuram", op. cit., p.48.

Cultivators (those engaged in cultivation, supervision or direction of cultivation land) constituted 20.04 per cent of the total workers in Gokilapuram. Agricultural labourers (wage-earning farm workers with no managerial or supervisory responsibilities) formed 59.97 per cent of the total work force. Workers in the 'other' category constituted 19.99 per cent of them.

The percentage of total workers in different occupations at the taluk level projected a similar picture with slight variations. About 57.30 per cent of the total workers were agricultural labourers and 18.32 per cent, cultivators. Nearly a quarter the work force came under the 'other' workers category.

The proportion of work force employed in the agricultural sector is generally large in India (68.7%).[4] Gokilapuram and Uthamapalayam taluk are no exceptions to it. Agricultural work force formed more than 75 per cent of the total labour force in them, while those involved in other economic activities were considerably lower.

2.4 Land Holdings and Land Utilisation Pattern

Land, a basic asset of an agrarian economy, is a pre-requisite for cultivation, the major source of income and an index of household status. It is associated with control over and access to other resources.[5] Table 2.7 records the distribution of operational land holdings by size in Gokilapuram during 1985-86.

TABLE 2.7: Distribution of Operational Land Holding by Size in Gokilapuram, 1985-86

Size of Holdings in Hectares	Number of Operational Holdings	Percentage to Total Holdings	Total Area Owned in Hectares	Percentage to Total Area Owned
0 – 0.5	72	15.55	19.44	5.60
0.5 – 1.0	316	68.25	160.49	46.23
1.0 – 2.0	46	9.94	51.98	14.97
2.0 – 3.0	14	3.02	29.54	8.51
3.0 – 4.0	5	1.08	15.35	4.42
4.0 – 5.0	4	0.86	16.40	4.72
5.0 – 7.5	1	0.22	5.63	1.62
7.5 – 10.0	2	0.43	15.14	4.36
10.0 – 20.0	3	0.65	33.21	9.57
Total	643	100.00	347.18	100.00

Source: Adangal, Gokilapuram, 1985-86.

The total number of operational land holdings in Gokilapuram were 463 in 1985-86. Jointly they owned 347.18 hectares of the total area. Over 83 per cent of the total operational holdings were less than one hectare. Together they owned only 51.83 per cent of the total holdings. About 14.9 per cent of the cultivating households held one to five hectares of land, accounting for 32.62 per cent of the total land. Less than one per cent of them owned five to 10 hectares of land. They held only 5.98 per cent of the total area. Between 10 to 20 hectares, 0.65 per cent holdings owned about 10 per cent of the operational area. This indicates that small cultivators form a significant component of the rural population in Gokilapuram. The Gini coefficient worked out for the village was 0.464, indicting inequality in the distribution of operational land holding in 1985-86. However, this was found to be relatively lower than the concentration ratios (Gini coefficient) at the state and all-India level, which were 0.64 and 0.629 respectively, during 1981-82.[6]

Table 2.8 projects the land utilisation pattern in Gokilapuram.

TABLE 2.8: Land Utilisation Pattern in Gokilapuram, 1985-86

Particulars	Area in Acres	Percentage to Total Geographical Area
A. Net Area Sown	782.65	75.64
B. Area Under Forests	–	–
C. Area not Available for Cultivation:		
(i) Land put to non-agricultural use	148.75	
(ii) Barren and Uncultivable land	5.00	
Total:	153.75	14.86
D. Other Cultivated Land excluding Fallow Land:		
(i) Permanent pastures and other grazing lands	–	–
(ii) Miscellaneous tree crops and groves not included in the net area sown	98.33	9.50
(iii) Cultivable waste	–	–
E. Fallow Lands:		
(i) Current	–	–
(ii) Fallow lands other than current fallow	–	–
F. Total Geographical Area	1034.74	100.00
G. Area Sown more than Once	742.38	
H. Total Area Cultivated	1525.03	

Source: *Adangal*, Gokilapuram, 1985-86.

The village has a geographical area of 1034.73 acres. The net area under cultivation was 782.65 acres (76%) in 1985-86. An area of 742.38 acres was sown more than once. This accounted for a total cropped area of 1525.03 acres during the year.

Nearly 15 per cent of the total area was unavailable for cultivation. Of it, 38 per cent was put to non-agricultural use. Barren and uncultivable land constituted less than half a percentage of the total area.

About 9.50 per cent of the total area came under miscellaneous tree crops and groves not included under the net area sown. There were no forests, permanent pastures and other grazing lands or fallow lands in the village.

Thus, Gokilapuram is found to be mainly an agrarian economy with nearly three-fourths of the total area under cultivation.

2.5 **Cropping Pattern**

Cropping pattern is strongly influenced by the year-round irrigation facilities. A wide range of crops are grown in the village. A glance at its cropping pattern would highlight the nature of the village agrarian economy. Table 2.9 gives an account of the area under different crops in Gokilapuram and Uthamapalayam taluk during 1985-86.

The data reveals that 96.82 per cent of the total cropped area in Gokilapuram was under food crops in 1985-86. On the other hand, only 3.17 per cent of it was under non-food crops. Of the total cropped area, over 94 per cent of land was covered by cereals alone. This indicates the dominance of food crop cultivation in the village.

In the taluk, 57.97 per cent of the total cropped area was under food crops, while non-food crops were cultivated in the remaining area. Under food crops, cereals constituted 40.72 per cent and pulses 8.69 per cent of the total cultivated land. Thus the proportion of food crop cultivation was relatively larger at the village and taluk level.

Unirrigated farming co-exists with a stable sector of high-yielding rice cultivation and a diversified commercial cropping in the village. Table 2.10 presents details on the principal crops grown in the irrigated and unirrigated areas of Gokilapuram during 1985-86.

In 1985-86, as much as 98.04 per cent of the total cropped area in Gokilapuram was irrigated, while only about two per cent (1.96) of it was unirrigated. In the unirrigated area, tamarind, sorghum (*cholam*), mango and silk cotton were grown.

TABLE 2.9: Area Under Different Crops in Gokilapuram and Uthamapalayam Taluk, 1985-86

Particulars	Gokilapuram: Area in Acres	Gokilapuram: Percentage to Total Cropped Area	Uthamapalayam Taluk: Area in Acres	Uthamapalayam Taluk: Percentage to Total Cropped Area
A. Area under Cereals and Pulses	1442.34	94.58	87198.41	49.41
(i) Total area under cereals	1442.34	94.58	71862.18	40.72
(ii) Total area under pulses	–	–	15336.23	8.69
(iii) Others	34.35	2.25	15106.52	8.56
B. Total Food Crop Area	1476.69	96.82	102304.93	57.97
C. Total-Non-Food Crop Area	48.34	3.17	74169.16	42.03
D. Total Food and Non-Food Crop Area	1525.03	100.00	176474.09	100.00

Source: Adangal, Gokilapuram, 1985-86.

TABLE 2.10: Area under Principal Crops in Gokilapuram, 1985-86

Crops	Area Irrigated in Acres	Unirrigated Area in Acres	Total Area in Acres	Percentage to Total Area
1. Paddy	1439.46	–	1439.46	94.38
2. Cholam (Sorghum)	–	2.88	2.88	0.19
3. Lime	0.30	–	0.30	0.02
4. Onion	1.95	–	1.95	0.13
5. Ladies Finger	0.30	–	0.30	0.02
6. Tomato	3.60	–	3.60	0.24
7. Mango	–	1.76	1.76	0.12
8. Banana	1.08	–	1.08	0.07
9. Kapas (Silk Cotton)	–	0.57	0.57	0.04
10. Tamarind	–	24.65	24.65	1.62
11. Coconut	48.48	–	48.48	3.18
Total	1495.17	29.86	1525.03	100.00

Source: Adangal, Gokilapuram, 1985-86.

Rice was the single principal food crop grown in the village. The total rice area accounted for more than 94 per cent of the total area sown. It occupied more than 96 per cent of the total irrigated area. Coconut was grown on about three per cent of the irrigated land. The crops grown in rest of the area were tomato, onion, ladies finger, lime and banana. The fruit and vegetable crops lagged far behind rice in terms of acreage under cultivation.

2.6 Rice Cultivation

Rice is the major crop cultivated in Madurai. Different varieties of rice are grown in the district. Table 2.11 lists the seasons suited for the cultivation of the principal rice varieties, as given by the 'crop production guide' for Madurai district.

TABLE 2.11: Seasons and Varieties of Rice Cultivation in Madurai District

Season	Varieties
1. Kar (May-June)	CO 37, CO 33, ADT 36, TKM 9, IR 50, JET 4786
2. Samba (August)	IR 20, Ponni, CO 43, CO 42, Madurai 2, Paiyur 1.
3. Late Samba-Thaladi (October-November)	IR 20, Ponni, CO 44, Madurai 2.
4. Navarai (December-January)	CO 37, CO 33, Rasi.

Source: Crop Production Guide, Horticulture and Oilseeds, Tamil Nadu Agricultural University and Directorates of Agriculture, TNAU, Coimbatore, 1985, p. 1.

There were 300 patta holders cultivating rice in Gokilapuram during 1985-86. Tenancy farming prevails in the region. The village has two crop seasons. The first season 'kharif' is sown in June-July and harvested in October-November and the second season 'rabi' is sown in October-November and harvested in March-April. During kharif, the rice farmers mainly cultivate IR 50 along with Jaya variety. The rice varieties generally grown in the second season are IR 20, CO 37, Nei Kichadi, Annapurna and Madurai 2. It is evident that majority of the rice farmers in the village have shifted completely to the production of high-yielding varieties. The sources of High-Yielding Varieties Seeds in the village are own stock, local purchase and government supplies.

Table 2.12 displays the variety-wise cultivation of rice by the Gokilapuram farmers in rabi 1985-86.

TABLE 2.12: Variety-wise Rice Cultivation in Gokilapuram, Rabi 1985-86

Rice Variety	Number of Farmers	Percentage to Total Farmers
1. IR 20	213	71.0
2. CO 37	54	18.0
3. Nei Kichadi	27	9.0
4. Madurai 2	4	1.3
5. Annapurna	2	0.7
Total	300	100.00

Source: *Adangal*, Gokilapuram, 1985-86.

About 71 per cent of the cultivators in the village grew IR 20 rice in rabi 1985-86. It was followed by CO 37, with 18 per cent of the farmers cultivating it. Nei Kichadi was produced by nine per cent of the rice growers. A very negligible percentage of them cultivated Madurai 2 and Annapurna rice varieties.

2.7 IR 20 and CO 37 Varieties of Rice

The high-yielding IR 20 rice variety was released by the International Rice Research Institute, Philippines. It was first introduced in India during 1965-66. Since its introduction, it has travelled a long way on the path of progress. It has contributed greatly to the stabilisation of rice yield in Tamil Nadu. Today, it is one of the most popular varieties of rice cultivated in many districts of the state.[7]

The rice variety CO 37, popularly known as *Vaigai*, is a locally bred high-yielding variety suited to the local conditions of Tamil Nadu. It was released in 1974 by the Paddy Breeding Station of Tamil Nadu Agricultural University, Coimbatore. It is popular among the rice farmers due to its shorter-duration of cultivation.

Table 2.13 furnishes particulars on the characteristic features of the two rice varieties selected for the study.

The duration of cultivating IR 20 rice variety is 130-135 days. It is well-known for its resistance to pest-attacks. The plant is semi-dwarf in size. The quality of rice is white, medium slender and fine. Its husk is straw coloured. Its average yield at the Research Station, Madurai, ranges between 6.5 to 7.0 tonnes per hectare.

TABLE 2.13: Particulars of Rice Varieties

Particulars	IR 20	CO 37
Parentage	IR 262 X TKM 6	TNI X CO 29
Duration (Days)	130 – 135	115
Average Yield (t/Ha)*	6.5 – 7.0	6.0 – 6.5
Grain Type	Medium slender	Medium
Morphological Characters:		
Habit	Semi-dwarf	Erect short
Husk Colour	Straw	Straw
Rice Colour	White	White
Grain Size (mm):		
Length	8.20	8.00
Breadth	2.70	2.90
Thickness	2.00	2.90

* Research Station Record, Tamil Nadu Agricultural University, Madurai, 1985-86.
Source: Crop Production Guide, op.cit., pp. 3-4.

CO 37 rice is a short-duration variety of 115 days. The plant is of erect short type. It produces white medium grains. It has field tolerance to pests and diseases. It tends to lodge under heavy rain. Its husk is also straw-coloured. Its average yield at the experimental station of Tamil Nadu Agricultural University, Madurai, is recorded to be 6.0 to 6.5 tonnes per hectare.

2.8 Other Infrastructural Facilities

Education

According to the 1981 Census, literacy rate in Gokilapuram was 48.19 per cent. This has been greater than the national (36.17%) and state (45.78%) literacy levels. Among persons, 61.53 per cent males and 34.30 per cent females were literates. This was also greater than the national literacy level of 46.74 per cent and 24.88 per cent respectively.[8] Thus, the literacy level in the village was higher than the national and state level figures.

The village has only one middle school. However, there are

schools in the neighbouring village of Rayappanpatty and a college at Uthamapalayam.[9]

Credit Facilities

The village has a wide credit coverage. It is served by a Cooperative Credit Society located at Uthamapalayam and a branch of Canara Bank situated in Rayappanpatty, about three kms away. Both these credit institutions provide short-term and medium-term loans. The Cooperative Agricultural Credit Society provides only crop loans. It gives short-term loans at an interest rate of 10.5 per cent and medium-term loans at 11 per cent per annum. The Canara Bank provides crop loans and jewel loans at the rate of interest of 10.5 per cent for short-term, and medium-term loans at 11.5 per cent per annum. The rate of interest at Canara Bank is slightly high. This is because it is basically a commercial banking institution unlike the Cooperative Society, which was organised solely to relieve rural indebtedness and promote thrift. Productive credit formed a major proportion of the loans taken by the villagers. The informal credit sector also functions side by side, charging a very high rate of interest. It flourishes mainly due to the urgent need of loans and need for consumption expenditure, especially among the poor.

Transport

The nearest bus-stand is nine kms away at Uthamapalayam and the nearest railway station is located at a distance of 40 kms at Bodi. The village is well-served by a good network of roads. Private and public transport co-exist, with frequent bus services connecting Gokilapuram to all the important neighbouring towns and villages. Taxi services are also available. Some of the landlords have their own cars. The nearest petrol and diesel oil station for the village is at Uthamapalayam.

Marketing

Processing facilities are available to the agriculturists at Uthamapalayam. The village does not have a co-operative marketing society service. The nearest marketing society is located 17 kms away at Chinnamanur. The markets for agricultural produce are the

Weekly Market at Cumbum (10 kms away) and the Mandi at Theni (40 kms away). The village lacks storage facilities. A major portion of the produce is sold within the village by the farmers. The Primary Agricultural Credit Society has a fair price retail shop in the village. Gokilapuram also has an active Milk Society. Most of the Integrated Rural Development Programme loans in the village are distributed through this society.

2.9 **Extension Services**

The village has an effective agricultural extension system. This has resulted in the wide-spread of agricultural information among the farmers in Gokilapuram. As a result, advanced techniques of agricultural production are followed by them. Chemical fertilizers, pesticides and high-yielding varieties of seeds are widely used. Although mechanisation is limited, farmers go in for it in the form of tractors.

2.10 **Integrated Rural Development Programme**

Since 1980, the Integrated Rural Development Programme (IRDP) is playing a major role in the development of villages through its anti-poverty programmes. The IRDP allocation has been substantial in the village. It contributes a major share to development expenditure. During 1983-85, more than Rs 4 lakhs had been distributed in Gokilapuram through this programme.[10]

2.11 **Rationale for the Selection of the Study Area and Rice Varieties**

Gokilapuram is one of the most important rice-producing regions in Uthamapalayam taluk. Endowed with fertile soil, it is an agriculturally progressive village. It possesses a stable and reliable system of irrigation. The village counts as a prime surface irrigated land in the entire Tamil Nadu state. The level of paddy productivity in Gokilapuram is relatively high, varying between 6.5 to 8.0 tonne per hectare, which has been sustained over the years.[11] A wide range of high value crops like cotton, coconut and banana are also grown in the village.

Agricultural extension service is quite effective in Gokilapuram.

Modern varieties of seeds are widely used with significant increase in yield in the village. There is almost a universal use of advanced agricultural techniques in terms of high-yielding seed varieties, chemical fertilizers and pesticides.

The village is provided with good infrastructural facilities. It has a good network of roads. Frequent buses and taxi services connect it to all the important neighbouring towns and villages. The Uthamapalayam block in general has a good coverage by financial institutions.

The expansion of commercial agriculture in terms of agricultural marketing and agro-based produce has resulted in the growth of a flourishing trade and commerce system in the Cumbum Valley. This has led to the expansion of agriculture-related activities in Gokilapuram. As a result its people are also engaged in varied types of business activity.

Agricultural labour constitutes a greater part of the total work force in the village. The labour force in the region displays quite high mobility. Daily or weekly intra-valley migration, seasonal migration and long-term migration to estates in other districts or states from the village are observed.

Thus, being one of the most progressive agrarian regions provided with an assured irrigation system in the taluk (even at the state level in the latter case) and considering the criteria of high adoption of high-yielding varieties seeds and technology with more than 94 per cent of the total cropped area under rice, Gokilapuram was particularly chosen for a study on irrigated high-yielding rice cultivation in the village.

In Indian agriculture, the relative importance of rice cultivation in rabi season is increasing in recent period. It is partly due to the rise in cropping intensity or multiple cropping in response to the increasing demand for agricultural produces. The introduction of high-yielding varieties has further increased its importance because the response of rice and other crops to modern technology is found to be greater in this season due to favourable weather.[12] Therefore, rabi season was considered suitable to evaluate the performance of the two selected rice varieties.

As IR 20 and CO 37 varieties were found to be popular among the rice farmers in Gokilapuram, the two high-yielding rice varieties were selected for a comparative study. Further, although CO 37 is a more recently introduced location-specific and shorter-duration hybrid variety compared to IR 20 rice (which was released by the International Rice Research Institute and is a longer-duration variety), the area under the latter variety is the largest not only in Madurai district, but also in the whole of Tamil Nadu. The same is seen in Gokilapuram too. Hence, it was deemed proper to examine the causes for the greater popularity of IR 20 compared to CO 37 variety among the rice farmers in the study area. Other related economic aspects of rice cultivation have also been investigated in the study.

2.12 Sample Design

The total rice farmers in the village were classified according to the variety cultivated and two ruling high-yielding varieties of rice (IR 20 and CO 37) were selected, based on their popularity in terms of the area covered and the total number of farmers cultivating it. Of the 300 rice growers in the study area, majority of them cultivated IR 20 variety while only 54 grew CO 37 variety in rabi 1985-86. Of the total IR 20 growers, a random sample of 100 farmers was drawn. In the case of CO 37 rice, dropping out four farmers for the reasons of their negligible size of operational holdings, 50 were selected. Thus, almost all farmers growing CO 37 in the rabi season were included and treated as a sample from a hypothetical population for the purpose of applying statistical tests.

As size of holding has a significant impact on the utilisation of farm inputs and the output produced, the sample farmers were further stratified into two groups by the size of operational holdings. Farmers cultivating less than five acres of land were grouped under the small farmers category, while those cultivating five acres and more were termed as large farmers. As per this definition, of the 100 sample farmers cultivating IR 20 rice, 74 were small farmers and the remaining 26, large farmers. Owing to the smaller number of farmers cultivating CO 37 rice, a similar classification in its case was not possible. Therefore, the CO 37 farmers were considered in total without any classification.

2.13 Study Period and Data Collection

The data collected pertains to the rabi seasons of the agricultural year 1985-86 of Gokilapuram village. The primary data for the study were collected using pre-tested questionnaire. The researcher visited the study area during the season under the study to collect the required information on the various socio-economic aspects relating to rice cultivation directly from the sample farmers. The format of the questionnaire used is given in the Appendix.

The necessary secondary data were obtained from the various Statistical Records of the Village Administrative Officer — Gokilapuram, Taluk Office and Assistant Director of Agriculture Office — Uthamapalayam, District Statistical Office — Madurai and the Census of India, 1981.

2.14 Measurement of Variables

This section gives the definition and measurement of the various variables, as used in the study.

1. *Land or Acreage* – The total physical area operated in acres by the farmers was taken into account. Rental value was calculated at the then prevailing market rate.
2. *Seeds* – The quantity of seeds purchased multiplied by its prevailing price per kilo gave the value of seeds.
3. *Labour* – Labour mandays was measured in terms of eight hours of work per day. It was evaluated in terms of the mandays worked by both male and female workers. As the average female wage rate was observed to be about half that of the male workers, two units of female labour was converted into one unit of male labour. Human labour included hired labour, permanent labour and family labour.

   Hired labour: It represented the labourers employed for farming activities during an agricultural season. The payments in cash and the imputed value of payments made in kind at the prevailing market price constituted their wages.

   Permanent labour: Labourers permanently hired for farming activities throughout the year represented permanent labour. Their wages were evaluated at the payments in cash and kind made at the prevailing market price.

   Family labour: In each family, only the members actively involved in farming activity were considered. It was valued at the same rate as hired labour at the prevailing market price during the season.

4. *Bullock Labour* – It comprised two bullocks and one male labourer. It included both hired and owned services. The value of only bullock service was computed at the prevailing market rate. The value of human labour was deducted from it. Bullock labour was calculated for eight hours of work per day.
5. *Organic Manure* – The value of organic manure was calculated in terms of the prevailing price for a cartload of manures. Each cartload contained about 150 kgs. of organic manure.
6. *Inorganic Fertilizer* – The value of inorganic fertilizer was computed by multiplying the prevailing price per kilo of each component of fertilizer required by their respective quantities used. The total expenditure on fertilizer divided by its quantity purchased gave the price per kilo.
7. *Pesticides* – The quantity of pesticides used multiplied by its prevailing price per kilo gave the value of pesticides. In the case of liquid pesticide, 1100 ml of it was considered equivalent to one kilo of pesticide used. The total expenditure on pesticide divided by its quantity purchased gave the average price per kilo. The commonly used pesticides were Monocrotopas, Endosulphan, Carbofuran, Phosmomidan, etc.
8. *Capital Flow* – It was measured as the sum of depreciation, opportunity cost and maintenance cost of the capital assets used for rice cultivation. Depreciation cost was obtained using the straightline method, while the opportunity cost was estimated at the prevailing rate of interest of the cooperatives.
9. *Yield* – It was measured in terms of the physical quantity of rice produced in kilos, as well as in its monetary value prevailing at the harvest time.
10. *Net Revenue* – It was obtained by deducting total cost (cost C) from the total income.
11. *Output per Manday* – Total output divided by the total number of mandays worked gave output per manday.
12. *Output per Acre* – Total output divided by the total farm size operated gave output per acre.
13. *Normalised Wage Rate* – Total labour cost divided by total mandays worked, divided by the prevailing price per kilo of rice gave normalised wage rate.
14. *Normalised Bullock Labour Price* – Total expenditure on bullock pairs divided by total bullock pair days employed, divided by the prevailing price per kilo of rice gave normalised

bullock pair day price.

15. *Normalised Fertilizer Price* – Total expenditure on inorganic fertilizer divided by its total quantity purchased, divided by the prevailing price per kilo of rice gave normalised fertilizer price.
16. *Normalised Pesticides Price* – Total expenditure on pesticide divided by its total quantity purchased, divided by the prevailing price per kilo of rice gave normalised pesticides price.
17. *Normalised Profit* – Total revenue minus total variable cost, divided by the prevailing price per kilo of rice gave normalised profit.

NOTES

1. R.N. Poduval, *Foodgrain Economy of Tamil Nadu: Problems and Prospects,* Emerald Publishers, Madras, 1987.
2. Commissioners of all Panchayat Unions, *District Statistical Hand Book for 1985-86,* Assistant Director of Statistics Office, Madurai, 1986, pp. 409-11.
3. Madhura Swaminathan, "Introduction", *Credit for Rural Development in Southern Tamil Nadu,* Tamil Nadu Agricultural University, September 1986, pp. 1-5.
4. S.K. Misra and V.K. Puri, "Labour Force, Occupational Structure and Urbanisation", *Indian Economy,* Himalaya Publishing House, Delhi, May 1986, p. 177.
5. Madhura, "The Setting: Gokilapuram", op.cit., p. 15.
6. T. Haque, "Temporal and Regional Variations in the Agrarian Structure in India", *Indian Journal of Agricultural Economics,* Vol. 42, No. 3, July-September 1987, pp. 313-318.
7. S. Rajasekaran, *Distinguishing Morphological Features of Rabi Rice Varieties,* State Level Training Programme on Rice Production Technology, Agricultural College and Research Institute, Tamil Nadu Agricultural University, Madurai, 19th-22nd November, 1984, p. 30.
8. "The Population", *Manorama Year Book,* (Ed.) K.M. Mathew, Manorama Publishing House, Kerala, 1987, p. 383.
9. Madhura, "The Setting: Gokilapuram", op. cit., p. 19.
10. *Ibid.*, "IRDP in Practice: A View from the Village", p. 111.
11. Op. cit., pp. 26-27.
12. C.H. Hanumantha Rao, "Technological Change and Fluctuations in Output", *Technological Change and Distribution of Gains in Indian Agriculture,* Macmillan Company of India Ltd., Delhi, 1975, p. 13.

CONCEPTS AND REVIEW OF LITERATURE

This chapter explains the main concepts used in the study. It also reports the major findings of some of the related studies undertaken for India and other countries, using similar methodology. However, although the techniques applied may be almost same, the results may differ due to the diversity within or between countries, their institutional environment, period of study, data base, specification of variables and the choice of different combinations of variables. Further, direction of enquiry of each study may be different depending on the importance of specific policy problems and data availability. Nevertheless, a brief review of related literature would be of great methodological interest. It would serve to illustrate a varying range of policy alternatives which have vital importance for resource use in agricultural development.

The main concepts discussed in this chapter are: (3.1) cost of cultivation, (3.2) yield gap, (3.3) farm size and productivity, and (3.4) economic efficiency.

Voluminous literatures are available on each of these subjects. Since it is too ambitious to include all of them in this chapter, only a few important related works are reviewed here. Besides, the review mainly focuses on studies relating to rice cultivation.

3.1 Cost of Cultivation

The relationship between cost and return is of crucial importance in agriculture. Cost of cultivation is an important determinant of price. In agriculture, cost of cultivation refers to the various input expenditures incurred by a farmer to attain the final produce. The nature of cost incurred by a farmer is of two kinds — (a) variable or operational cost, and (b) fixed cost.

Variable cost is the cost incurred by a farmer on factors of production such as seeds, human labour, fertilizers, pesticides, bullock labour, livestock feed, tractor fuel, etc. On the other hand, fixed cost is the cost incurred on rent, taxes, depreciation of implements and machinery, interest, insurance premium, etc. The former varies with changes in the quantity of output produced, while the latter remains constant over time and does not vary with changes in the levels of output. In the process of cultivation, variable cost is the driving factor which determines how much and what is to be produced. Fixed cost helps to make important decisions on the technological practice to be adopted and the quantity of output to be produced. Fixed cost exists even in the absence of cultivation, while variable cost does not.

The Farm Management Studies[1] in India broadly classifies cost of cultivation into: (i) Cost A_1, (ii) Cost A_2, (iii) Cost *B*, and (iv) Cost *C*. The following are the items included under each of them.

1. *Cost* A_1:

(a) Value of hired labour (permanent and casual),
(b) Value of owned bullock labour,
(c) Value of hired bullock labour,
(d) Value of owned machinery,
(e) Hired machinery charges,
(f) Value of fertilizers,
(g) Value of manure (owned and purchased),
(h) Value of seed (both farm produced and purchased),
(i) Value of insecticides and pesticides,
(j) Irrigation charges (both owned and hired machines),
(k) Canal water charges,
(l) Land revenue, cesses and other taxes,
(m) Depreciation on farm implements (both bullock drawn and used by human labour),
(n) Depreciation on farm buildings, farm machinery and irrigation structure,
(o) Interests on working capital, and
(p) Miscellaneous expenses (artisans, ropes and repairs to small farm implements).

2. *Cost* A_2: It includes Cost A_1, and

(q) Rent paid for leased-in land.

3. *Cost B*: It includes Cost A_2, and

(r) Imputed rental value of owned land (less land revenue paid there upon), and
(s) Imputed interest on fixed capital (excluding land).

4. *Cost C*: It includes Cost *B*, and

(t) Imputed value of family labour.

Cost A_1 is incurred by a farmer when he is the owner and contributes his own land and other resources. Cost A_2 is the tenant cost incurred by him when all the land is leased-in and rent has to be paid for it. Cost *B* is incurred when, in addition to the above costs, imputed interest is paid on owned fixed capital. Cost *C* is incurred when the imputed cost of family labour is also included. It is the most comprehensive cost.

In their study on the cost and returns of principal crops in the districts of Tamil Nadu, Rajagopalan, et al.,[2] considered only Cost *A* (variable) and Cost *C* (fixed). The two cost concepts included the following components:-

1. *Cost A*:

(i) Value of human labour, including family labour,
(ii) Value of bullock labour,
(iii) Value of machinery charges,
(iv) Value of seed,
(v) Value of insecticide,
(vi) Value of manures and fertilizers,
(vii) Cost of irrigation, and
(viii) Interest on working capital.

2. *Cost C*:

Cost *A* + rent (including rent paid by the tenant or rental value of owned land) + interest on fixed capital, excluding land + land revenue, cesses and taxes + depreciation of implements and machinery.

Cost *C* was computed from Cost *A*, assuming that the latter accounts for 70 per cent of the total cost. This is a highly arbitrary assumption.

In the present study, Cost *A* (variable cost) and Cost *C* (fixed cost) are considered for the analysis of the cost structure of rice cultivation. The two categories of cost include the following items:-

1. *Cost A*:

(i) Human labour including family labour,
(ii) Bullock labour,
(iii) Chemical fertilizers,
(iv) Pesticides,
(v) Seeds cost,
(vi) Farm manures,
(vii) Cost of irrigation, and
(viii) Interest on working capital.

2. *Cost C*:

(ix) Rent, and
(x) Interest on fixed capital excluding land revenue, cess and taxes, and depreciation of implements and machinery.

The assumption of Cost *A* constituting 70 per cent of the total cost has been ruled out in this study. Instead, Cost *A* and Cost *C* were worked out separately for each rice variety and the farmer groups.

The following are the important findings of some of the studies on cost and return structure of rice cultivation, conducted in the context of India and other countries. The review would provide a better understanding of the concept.

The changes in cost and return structure of high-yielding (IR 8) versus local varieties of rice per acre in Ferozepur district of Punjab were examined by Hanumantha Rao.[3] The analysis was based on the Farm Management Data for 1969-70. The study revealed a significant reduction in unit costs and a rise in the share of profits under the high-yielding varieties technology. The new technology turned out to be cost-saving on three factors – land, labour and capital (fixed and variable), though the greatest cost-saving was on land followed by labour. However, a significant decline was observed in the unit cost of fertilizers. The greater fall in labour cost compared to capital cost indicated a rise in the overall capital-labour ratio, despite a reduction in the ratio of fixed capital to labour. This rise in the capital-labour ratio was attributed essentially to the increase in fertilizer use. For high-yielding varieties of rice, the expenditure on current inputs constituted 48.6 per cent of the total cost, as against 41.9 per cent for the local variety.

Cost and returns of principal crops in the different districts of Tamil Nadu were analysed by Rajagopalan, et al.[4] The state was classified into eight zones. A fixed number of taluks was selected with probability proportional to the area under the principal crops in the zone to the total area of the crops in the whole state. A three-stage stratified random sampling technique was adopted with taluk as the primary, three villages as the secondary and 10 operational holdings as the ultimate unit. Data were collected from the sample farmers for the year 1976-77. Here, the distribution of input cost for raising high-yielding and improved varieties of paddy and returns per hectare in Madurai district are only considered.

In Madurai, human labour occupied a major share in total cost. Its percentage share was greater for high-yielding varieties (36.52) compared to the improved varieties (34.72) of paddy. Fertilizer and manures occupied the next position, its percentage ranging from 27.43 per cent for improved variety to 24.59 per cent for high-yielding varieties. It was followed by irrigation cost. The share of pesticides was the lowest among input costs under both the varieties.

The yield per hectare of high-yielding varieties was 27.85 quintals, while it was 26.15 quintals for the improved varieties. Their input-output ratios were 2.01 and 1.92 respectively. The cost-benefit ratio was 0.41 for high-yielding varieties and 0.34 for improved paddy. Variable cost and total cost per hectare were respectively Rs. 1738.81 and Rs. 2484.11 for high-yielding varieties and Rs. 1600.78 and Rs. 2286.74 for improved varieties. The gross returns and net returns were also greater for the high-yielding varieties. This indicated that despite higher cost of production, cultivation of high-yielding varieties was more profitable compared to the improved varieties.

A study of the adoption and yield differentials of high-yielding varieties and local paddy in Hospet (Bellary district), Bhadravathi (Shimoga district) and Mandya (Mandya district) taluks of Karnataka state was undertaken by Singh and Govindaraju.[5] The data used pertained to the summer and kharif seasons of 1974-75. A random sample of 55, 40 and 45 were respectively drawn from two representative villages of Hospet, Bhadravathi and Mandya. In the former two taluks, the adoption rate of high-yielding variety paddy was high, while in the latter it was low.

Paddy cultivation was found to be more profitable in Hospet than in Bhadravathi or Mandya. The differential performance of paddy crops among taluks was attributed to the difference in the intensity of fertilizer use. The high-yielding variety performed much better in summer while the local varieties did better in kharif. The cost of production and cost-output ratios revealed the cultivation of high-yielding varieties to be more economical than the traditional ones. So a more judicious use of canal water was suggested in summer to increase the area under the former variety.

The pattern of input used was almost similar in the taluks cultivating high-yielding varieties, while it differed considerably for the taluk cultivating local varieties. In the cost structure, operating cost accounted for about three-fourths of the total cost. Land followed by fertilizer were the most important items of cost in all the taluks. Surprisingly, the share of human labour was relatively lower in them. The shares of land and land-augmenting inputs such as fertilizer, manures and seeds together were more than 74 per cent in Mandya, 59 per cent in Hospet and 62 per cent in Bhadravathi. The productivity of paddy was the highest in Mandya, followed by Hospet and Bhadravathi. This could be due to the more intensive use of land-augmenting inputs and more suitable atmospheric condition in the taluk.

The profit per acre for aggregate paddy crop was greater in Hospet than in Mandya, despite the more intensive use of inputs in the latter. Profits were considerably lower in Bhadravathi. The ratio of total cost of output for producing one rupee worth of output was 47, 63 and 65 paise, respectively. It was inferred that cultivation of high-yielding varieties of paddy was more economical, despite its lower yield per acre compared to the local varieties.

Small farmers were not only equally good at adopting the new technology of paddy, but they also made greater or equally intensive use of the modern inputs. Their productivity per acre was relatively higher than on large farms. This inference is relevant here, as rice cultivation requires quite close supervision and intensive use of labour which declines with the expansion in farm size.

The per hectare use of material inputs for all crop production, including rice, was compared for the mid-'50s (pre-technological change period) and early '70s, i.e., 1969-73 (post-technological change period), by Ghosh.[6] Aggregated Farm Management Survey data for Hooghley district in West Bengal were used for the analysis. It was observed that material inputs such as chemical fertilizers, oil cakes, other organic manures and insecticides and pesticides which were virtually non-existent in the '50s, were used in remarkable quantities in the early '70s by the farmers. The increase in the use of inputs over the years was noteworthy. The total variable cost as a percentage to total expenditure increased from 54.2 per cent in 1969-70 to more than 65 per cent in the early '70s.

Harrison[7] studied the cost and return structure of small and large farmer groups in Tanjore district of Tamil Nadu. Data were collected for ADT 27 paddy cultivation in the Kuruvai season (June-October), 1967-68. A multi-stage (stratified) random sampling technique was adopted to collect details on farm management. About 10 farms from each of the 15 villages were selected, giving a total sample of 150 farmers.

The study revealed that small farmers cultivated ADT 27 more extensively than the large farmers. The former planted more than 50 per cent of their net operated area with the rice, while the latter planted only about 39 per cent of it. There was also a greater intensity of landuse by the small growers than the larger ones. On an average, small farmers used about 22 per cent more labour per hectare than the large farmers. More intensive use of family labour accounted for most of this difference. Use of other variable inputs by the two farmer groups tended to follow a similar pattern. Small farmers spent a greater amount per hectare on the inputs. For both size groups, chemical fertilizer was the most important variable expenditure, with seeds running a close second.

The physical performances of two location-specific modern varieties (ADT 31 and CO 37) were compared with an exotic variety (IR 20) by Kalirajan[8] over the kharif season of May-June 1977, in a progressive village of Gobichetty block in Coimbatore district, Tamil Nadu. Data were gathered from a random sample of 41 farmers each, growing location-specific and exotic varieties in irrigated areas. The per acre average input use, yield and size of holding for the sample farmers showed that both the groups used similar levels of inputs, yet, the average yields of the location-specific varieties (2.68 tonnes per acre) were significantly higher than that of the exotic variety (1.77 tonnes per acre). This reflected the superiority of location-specific varieties in increasing paddy production. It also suggested that there was scope for increasing paddy production substantially through location-specific varieties, without changing the infrastructure.

Fujimoto[9] studied rice farming by the Malay and Chinese farmers under the same natural conditions and farm environment of the Northern district of Province of Wellesley in Malaysia. Data were collected for the 1977-78 main season, from two Malay and one Chinese village. A complete survey was conducted in the two Malay villages (85 farmers), while a sampling survey was undertaken in the Chinese village (25 farmers). Farm management data were used to examine the input-output and cost and return relationships.

Marked differences existed between the two groups in terms of farm management and the resulting average yield per acre. The average amount of labour input per acre was significantly greater for Malays than for the Chinese. The latter used larger quantities of cash inputs like fertilizer and pesticides per acre. Farm management was generally observed to be capital-intensive among the Chinese and labour-intensive among the Malays. The average yield per acre was significantly different for the two groups, with the Chinese reaping greater yield than the Malays.

To further clarify the differences in farm management of the two groups, a comparative study of their cost and return structure was undertaken. The average production costs were lower for the Chinese than for the Malays. The differences were mainly caused by labour cost, rent and interest on farm assets. The most important cost component was interest on farm assets, which constituted 36 per cent of the total cost among the Malays and 50 per cent among the Chinese. This trend was due to the high value of land, which formed a major part of the total farm assets. Labour cost formed 38 per cent of the total cost among the Malays and 31 per cent among the Chinese. The average rent was higher for the Malays, as the incidence of tenancy was greater among them. On an average, both groups recorded negative net revenue which was attributed to the inclusion of payment to capital and family labour. Excluding them, the average income was higher for Chinese than for the Malays. Eventhough the difference in rice income was not particularly large on a per acre basis, the difference in farm size affected the total income from rice for both groups.

3.2 Yield Gap

Agricultural scientists evolved High-Yielding Varieties with the object of solving food problems prevailing in parts of the world, through increase in productivity rather than expansion in the area cultivated. It involves the transfer of research from experimental laboratories to the farm. Agricultural research centres strive to maximise yield through optimum use of resources. These centres seek to develop technologies suitable to the socio-economic conditions of a region, through integrated socio-economic and biological research. The validity and viability of experiment findings are examined by undertaking on-farm testing, demonstrations, operational research projects, etc. However, the farmers' yields are often reported to be lower than those obtained at the experimental stations.[10] This difference between the experiment station yield and the actual farm yield is referred to as 'Yield Gap'.[11]

There are two common ways of defining the concept of yield gap. First, directly comparing the experiment station yield to the yield at farm. Second, comparing yield of the best farm with that of the average or the poorest farm.[12] Thus, yield gap may be classified into two kinds – yield gap I and yield gap II. The Yield gap I represents the difference between experiment station yield and potential farm yield. The Yield gap II corresponds to the potential farm yield and actual farm yield. The maximum yield obtainable from a variety under a particular situation is called 'potential yield', while the average yield attained under farm conditions is known as the 'actual yield'. The factors that prevent farmers from achieving the potential yield under farmers' conditions are known as 'yield constraints'.

There are three kinds of constraints[13] which cause yield gap. They are – (1) environmental constraints, (2) biological constraints, and (3) socio-economic constraints. Environmental constraints are caused by – (i) environmental differences, and (ii) non-transferable technology. Experiment stations are usually located in places ideal for farming, whereas the same is not true of farmers' fields. Moreover, there are hardly any cost or input constraints at these centres, while farmers often encounter such problems at farm level. Above all, some of the techniques adopted at the experiment station may not be transferable to a farmers's field. These constraints cause Yield gap I.

Biological constraints include: (i) variety, (ii) weeds, (iii) diseases and insects, (iv) problem soil, (v) irrigation facilities, and (vi) soil fertility. By and large, these constraints arise from the non-application of the required inputs. Experiment stations may not face such problems, while farmers often face them at the farm level.

Socio-economic constraints arise from: (i) costs and returns, (ii) credit problems, (iii) tradition and attitudes, (iv) knowledge, and (v) input availability and institutional facilities. It is the outcome of these constraints which prevent farmers from adopting the technology as recommended. A farmer may consider the economic viability of following the new technology in terms of its costs and returns. Some farmers may not like to give up their traditional practices. Moreover, some aspects of the technology may not be understood by them. It also results from the lack of institutional facilities like non-availability of inputs, credits, etc. Biological and socio-economic constraints together contribute towards Yield gap II.

Yield gap analysis becomes instrumental in measuring the magnitude of gap in the yields and in the identification of constraints responsible for it. It is not proper to consider Yield gap I in a study, as experiment stations rarely encounter the constraints experienced by the farmers. Such estimates would be biased and larger than what it is actually under the farmers' conditions.[14] Hence, Yield gap II has been examined in the study. It was defined as the difference between the highest yield obtained by the most efficient farmer in the sample and the average level of yield achieved under farmers' conditions.

Many studies have identified yield gap by defining it in different ways. The main findings of some of the studies conducted by various researchers are reported here. Besides, a brief review of studies relating to the determinants of yield are also presented. It would provide an insight into the determinants of yield and yield gap under different conditions in different regions of the country and the world.

Mukherji[15] estimated the yield gap ratios in rice production during the 1975-76 kharif season. He observed farmers' technical competence to be high when the gap ratio was low and vice-versa. High yield gap was reported in states like Bihar and Orissa. This was attributed to the fact that while the demonstration plots were situated in irrigated areas, rice at the farms were generally produced under rain-fed conditions.

Flinn and Ali[16] studied the yield gap in two villages of Gujranwala district, Pakistan, using data collected from a random sample of 115 farmers. The mean yield of Basmati variety was found to be 1.8

tonnes per hectare over the sampled farms during the 1982 rice crop. The yield of rice in the study area ranged from 0.6 to 3.0 tonnes per hectare. Thus, a yield gap of over one tonne per hectare was identified between the average and the highest farm yield. This suggested that, given current technology, there were opportunities for increasing rice yields in the study area.

Davidson and Martin[17] surveyed the variations in yields on farms and at experiment station for different crops, including rice, in Australia. The yield gap between farms and experiment station was observed to vary according to the cultivation season. During good years, the yield at experiment station was found to increase more rapidly than the yield on farms within the same district. This was mainly because the farmers were more interested in maximising their profits by limiting their input investment, while the experimenters only aimed at maximising yield and had no cost restraints.

Sadhu and Mahajan[18] used Cobb-Douglas type of production function to estimate the elasticities of output with respect to inputs in paddy cultivation in Marh (Jammu district in Jammu and Kashmir) and Batala (Gurudaspur district in Punjab) blocks. A random sample of 150 farmers were selected from three villages of each block, for the agricultural year 1976-77. The sample was stratified into small, medium and large farm groups. Value of paddy yield was the dependent variable, while the four independent variables selected were cropped area, human labour, bullock labour and value of yield increasing technology comprising fertilizers, manures and working expenses. The regression models were first run separately for the total sample of each block and then separately for the three farm groups.

In the case of both blocks, the coefficients of land and yield increasing technology were positive and statistically significant. The coefficient of human labour emerged negative, which may be attributed to the excessive employment of labour. The coefficient of bullock labour was negative and significant for Batala, but positive and insignificant for Marh. However, the authors did not explain the varying behaviours of the variable in the two blocks. The four variables caused about 95 per cent of the variations in paddy output of the two blocks.

The analysis of production functions for different farm size groups of the two blocks revealed a positive and significant relationship between land and output in all the three cases. The elasticities of labour emerged similar to that in the pooled analysis of all paddy farms. The regression coefficients of bullock labour were negative for all farm sizes in Batala but, negative in Marh on medium and large farms. In both cases, yield increasing technology emerged positive for all farm groups, excepting the small farmers of Batala. The variables explained more than 80 per cent of the variations in all cases except medium size farms of Marh block, where the variation was only 39 per cent. However, the cause for the lower value of R^2 was not explained by the authors.

Using the Farm Management data for 1955-56, Saini[19] examined the efficiency of rice farmers in the allocation of resources. The study covered 200 farms of 100 each, in the districts of Meerut and Muzaffarnagar in Uttar Pradesh. Cobb-Douglas production function was fitted with output as the dependent variable and area, labour, bullock labour, farm manures and fertilizers and irrigation as the five independent variables. The included explanatory variables together caused 79 per cent of the variations in the output of paddy. The analysis indicated that output was highly responsive and significantly related to land, followed by human labour. Bullock labour also had a positive and significant impact on output. The elasticity was positive but quite low for manures and fertilizer. Irrigation showed a negative response, due to the excessive rainfall during the year which affected the crop badly.

Kalirajan and Shand[20] studied the stability of yield parameter between location-specific varieties (ADT 31 and CO 37) and exotic varieties (IR 20), using a multiple regression model with intercept and slope dummy variables. All the 41 farmers growing exotic varieties and a random sample of 50 location-specific varieties growers in Seyyampalayam village of Coimbatore district were selected for the study. Data were collected for the summer season (kharif) of 1977.

The regression analysis showed that all coefficients were positive and significant. The low values of the estimates indicated that in response to an increase in the application of these inputs, yields of the two varieties would increase only by small amounts. The most important finding was the significance of BPH (Brown Plant Hopper) control factor, which was different for location-specific varieties and the exotic varieties. Pesticides were used by both the farmers as preventive and curative measure, as recommended by the extension officials. The highly significant coefficient of BPH control for location-specific varieties implied that its effective control increased net yield by 21 per cent, whereas for exotic variety, it increased by only 11 per cent. This difference arose out of the difference in maturation period of the exotic variety which coincided with the build-up of the pest. Consequently, the recommended methods of pest management also failed to control BPH effectively.

Using a linear regression equation, the relationship between yield and factors such as fertilizer, weed control cost, distance of the parcel from the turn-out, land tenure and rice variety was studied by Adulavidhaya, and others.[21] The data for the analysis were obtained from one parcel each of 165 farms for the 1974 wet season and from one parcel each of 141 farms in the 1975 dry season of Suphan Buri province in Thailand. During the wet season, a weak relationship was identified between yield and fertilizer and variety. However, there was no impact of weed control or tenure on yield. In the dry season, only fertilizer had a significant impact on yield. Rice variety was not included as a variable in this season, as only modern varieties were grown then. Other independent variables were not significantly related to yield.

Kuo, Wu and Li[22] attempted to identify the factors associated with variations in yield, using a regression model. Data were collected from a sample of 60 farmers of Tah-Yia, Taiwan in 1975. Fertilizer, labour, net returns, technician's value and number of practice constituted the main explanatory variables. The analysis showed that the independent variables explained 51 per cent of the observed variability in rice yield. Net return, representing economic incentive, was the most significant factor affecting the yield of rice. It was followed by fertilizer, technician's value and number of practices, which were all positively and significantly related to yield. The result suggested that more extension services were needed in rice production. They also indicated that natural manure, complementary irrigation and hand-weeding had positive effect on rice yields.

Datta and others[23] estimated the relationship between rice growth and 32 socio-economic variables, using data for 1974 wet season to 1977 dry season of Nueva Ecija in Philippines. The independent variables together explained 66 per cent of the observed variability in yield. About 11 variables were significantly related to rice growth. Water stress, which substantially reduces yield at farm, did not exercise any significant effect. Soil texture emerged highly significant although it was not expected to influence yield much.

A regression model was estimated by Wu, Kuo and Li,[24] to measure the effect of production inputs on rice yield. Data were collected from 60 sample farms in Taichung, Taiwan, for the first rice crop season in 1977. The seven selected independent variables (labour, manure, insecticide, herbicide, fertilizer, density and damage reported) explained only 33 per cent of the variations in yield. Damage by natural forces was reported to be the most significant factor affecting yield. Only fertilizers and herbicides had positive and significant impact on it.

To delineate the cultivation practices of Malay and Chinese farmer groups, Fujimoto[25] analysed the determinants of rice yield with respect to cultivation techniques, using a regression model. The functional relationship between yield and four independent variables – labour, fertilizer, pesticides and farmers' educational level – was estimated using the data for 1977-78 main season of Wellesley Province in Malaysia.

The analysis revealed that 41 per cent and 63 per cent of the variations in yield among the Malay and Chinese farmers respectively, were jointly explained by the independent variables. Education was the most important determinant of yield in both groups. However, its influence on Chinese was significantly greater than on the Malays. It emphasized the role of technical knowledge in the determination of rice incomes. Next, pesticide exercised a significant impact on yield in both cases. Even if price uncertainties and production risks were accounted for, increase in pesticide application appeared to be a highly desirable method of raising productivity among the two farmers. While the contribution of fertilizer was positive and significant for the Malays, it was negative and insignificant for the Chinese. In the former case, it implied a greater increase in yield than its additional cost, justifying its increased use. On the other hand, the Chinese seemed to have already used large quantities of fertilizer, its further increase resulting in an insignificant effect on yield. The insignificant coefficient of hired labour for the Malays indicated that the use of labour (mainly family labour) was already so intensive that any additional employment would only have an insignificant effect on the yield level. In contrast, its influence was positive and significant for the Chinese. This suggested that yield could be increased through additional days of hired labour.

The findings indicate that different technical improvements are required to raise the levels of yield for different farm groups. It is also clear that differences in production attitudes, farm management and institutional arrangements are reflected in the actual process of farm operations and the resulting average yield per acre.

3.3 Farm Size and Productivity

One among the many controversial issues in agriculture is the relationship between farm size and farm efficiency. The bone of contention with respect to farm size and productivity has been the nature of relationship that exists between the two variables. Various economic researchers have defined the two concepts in different terms and have arrived at different conclusions for different regions, at different periods of time (especially, before and after the introduction of High-Yielding Varieties technology). Yet, there is no unanimity in the conclusions derived by them.

Basically two main types of relationship between farm size and farm efficiency have been identified. They are: – (i) inverse or negative relationship, and (ii) direct or positive relationship. The concept of inverse relationship postulates that as farm size increases, farm efficiency declines. Direct relationship proclaims an increase in farm efficiency in response to an increase in farm size. An identification of the nature of relationship between farm size and productivity would provide important implications on land reform and land ceiling policies relevant to the nature of relationship that prevails in the area under study.

The concept of farm size and farm efficiency may be defined in different terms. According to Khusro, "Farm size can be defined either in terms of a single input, say, acreage or in terms of output; and farm efficiency either in terms of output per unit of a single input, acreage, or as output per unit of cost of all inputs".[26]

Farm size, measured in acreage, is one of the critical and crucial inputs. It is an input which cannot be concealed. However, problems arise when yield of different kinds of land (i.e., good, bad, dry, wet, etc.) are compared. This can be overcome by a method of standardisation, which is also not entirely free from arbitrariness. Despite these problems, acreage is a highly satisfactory measure of farm size.

On the other hand, output is a more general measure of farm size. "The simplest measure of output may appear to be in physical weight or volume. But this is, too obviously, an unsatisfactory measure as it equates high income yielding and low income yielding crops as well as varieties of crops and takes no account of their differential value".[27] If output is measured in terms of value, it entails problems of inter-temporal comparisons, index number problems and the imputational difficulties of values for retained output, etc. However, output is also used as a variable to represent farm size.

Farm efficiency or productivity has been interpreted in different ways by different researchers. Hanumantha Rao[28] defined farm efficiency in terms of output per acre, which represents land productivity. Khusro[29] defined efficiency as gross output per acre, farm business income per acre and net profit per acre. According to him, total cost comprises paid-out cost (variable cost) and retained cost (i.e., costs for farm produced inputs like family labour, owned land and farm-produced capital representing imputed costs). Net farm business income indicated the difference between the value of gross output and paid-out cost (inclusive of depreciation). He believed that more than trying to maximise gross output (a return which does not wholly accrue to the farmer), a farmer would be more interested in maximising his farm business income. Net profit was computed by deducting retained cost from net farm business income.

Raj Krishna[30] defined the concept in terms of output per acre, output per manday, average variable cost and average total cost. The four variables indicate the index of returns and payments. The former two represent the crucial and relevant variables that influence farm decisions. Output per acre and output per manday respectively represent land and labour productivity which a farmer would seek to maximise, while average variable cost and average total cost represent the factors which he would like to minimise.

In the present study, farm size is defined in terms of acreage or land cultivated by a farmer. Factors – output per acre, output per manday, average variable cost and average total cost, respectively, represent farm efficiency. The four variables were particularly selected to define farm efficiency, as they indicate the factors which farmers would strive to maximise and minimise. The following are some of the brief reviews on studies relating to the concepts of farm size and farm efficiency and inequalities in income distribution. They would provide an idea on the nature of relationship between farm size and farm efficiency and also on the inequalities in distribution of income under Indian conditions.

Hanumantha Rao[31] analysed the relationship between farm size and output per acre under the traditional technology in the '50s and under the adoption of the new techniques in the late '60s in areas of the fastest change with regard to wheat and rice, viz., Muzaffarnagar (Uttar Pradesh), Ferozepur (Punjab) and West Godavari (Andhra Pradesh).

Inverse relationship between farm size and output per acre was identified under the traditional technology. The relationship was statistically significant in the '50s in Muzaffarnagar and West Godavari and in 1955-56 in Ferozepur. With the adoption of new inputs in the mid-'60s, a weakening in the inverse relationship was observed in Muzaffarnagar. Over the transition period, the regression coefficient progressively reduced from –0.25 in 1955-56 to –0.04 in 1968-69. The relationship was statistically significant for Muzaffarnagar, while it was insignificant in the latter period in Ferozepur and West Godavari. The weakening or disappearance of the inverse relationship between farm size and output per acre implied a higher rate of growth of output among large farms when compared to small farms. This was achieved by large farmers not through greater application of labour input per acre, but through the greater use of capital inputs or the increasing substitution of capital for labour.

Raj Krishna[32] examined the relationship between farm size and farm efficiency in Ferozepur and Amritsar districts of Punjab, on the basis of simple linear regression and quadratic equations. The 1956-57 Farm Management Studies data were used for the analysis. By stratified sampling method, 200 holdings (with 10 each from 20 villages) were selected.

The analysis revealed a weak relationship between farm size (in terms of acreage and output) and the efficiency variables (in terms of output per acre, output per manday, average variable cost and average total cost). None of the eight linear relations explained more than 13 per cent of the variations in productivity or cost. All the eight relations were also tested for deviation from linearity. The analysis showed that all relations except output per acre and land, output per manday and land and average total cost and land were significantly deviant from linearity.

Chattopadhyay and Rudra[33] studied the relationship between farm size and productivity on the basis of disaggregated data collected by Farm Management Survey, for different regions in India, at selected points of time. Their study consisted of four sections. In the first part, they observed the relationship between farm size and productivity in some of the latest statistical works of others. In the second part, they discussed the results relating to farm size and productivity based on grouped data. In the third part, they approached the relationship through 'cheap labour based-explanation' advanced by A.K. Sen. In the fourth part, they presented their understanding of the alleged relationship. They formulated nine hypotheses in their study, which were tested. They concluded, "As such, our results do not claim any definitive refutation or confirmation of hypothesis for the country as a whole".

Chattopadhyay and Rudra[34] studied the relationship between farm size and productivity on the basis of Farm Management data for different regions in India, such as Uttar Pradesh (1966-69), Andhra (1967-70), Punjab (1954-57), Orissa (1967-70), Assam (1968-71) and Tamil Nadu (1967-70). They found that as farm size increased, yield per unit of land decreased in all the regions. As far as West Bengal (1954-57 and 1970-73) and Kerala (1962-65) were concerned, productivity remained unchanged in relation to size. Observing the pattern of relationship between farm size and productivity, they came to the conclusion that negative relation may hold true in certain parts of the country at certain times, but not everywhere and at all times.

Rudra and Sen[35] reviewed various articles relating to farm size and productivity in Indian agriculture. They examined Ashok Rudra's study based on disaggregated data from Farm Management Survey, wherein he had concluded that the inverse relationship between farm size and productivity is not a confirmed phenomenon. He had categorically stated that relationship between yield and farm size is spurious. On the whole, he raised doubts on the universal validity of the inverse relationship. Based on the review, Rudra and Sen concluded that the current policy discussions have concentrated only on small-scale peasant farming and large-scale capitalist farming, while the third alternative of cooperative farming is totally ignored. They concluded that, "A revival of decisions on farm size, production model and resource-use in Indian agriculture can contribute substantially only if the choices are not artificially restricted. The problems, deep-rooted as they are, call for the examination of far-reaching solutions, going well-beyond institutional forms already common in Indian agriculture".

The relationship between farm size and farm efficiency was

analysed by Khusro[36] for two districts each in seven selected states (viz., Andhra Pradesh, Bombay, Madhya Pradesh, Madras, Punjab, Uttar Pradesh and West Bengal). The Farm Management Studies data used were averaged for three years, i.e., 1954-55, 1955-56 and 1956-57, in the hope that a three-year-average may have greater reliability than the one-year figures. The change in returns per acre (efficiency) was analysed in response to the change in acreage (farm size). Efficiency was examined in terms of gross output, net farm business income and net profits respectively.

The relationship was first studied in terms of changes in per farm returns to changes in acreage. The analysis revealed that as acreage expanded, per farm gross output, farm business income and net profits increased in all the states. Next instead of per farm returns, efficiency was examined in terms of per acre returns. The results showed that as farm size expanded, gross output and farm business income per acre declined for all states (except in Uttar Pradesh), while net profits increased. The result generalised for Indian farming (obtained by averaging the states' data) in the 1950s, confirmed the individual state-wise results. The phenomena of decreasing gross output per acre and farm business income per acre were explained by the possibility that as farm size expands, the proportion of bad and indifferent land increases. This ultimately accounts for the decrease in per acre output and farm income.

The relationship was once again estimated by correcting acreage to an index of fertility, representing output or land revenue. The analysis revealed that in almost all states, land revenue per acre declined with an expansion in farm size. This confirmed the hypothesis of decreasing soil fertility. However, Khusro's use of land revenue figures as an indicator of fertility attracted strong criticisms, since land revenue is regarded as a poor index of fertility. The relationships of the three efficiency factors to corrected acreage indicated that in the Indian farming of the 1950s, gross output and farm business income per corrected acre had no general tendency to increase or decrease, while net profit per acre increased with farm size, starting from a negative response for small farms and rising to a positive one.

In sum, the result showed that whether farm size is judged by standardised acreage or output and whether efficiency is measured by farm business income (or paid-out cost) per standard acre or paid-out cost per unit of output or income, constant returns to scale prevailed everywhere among the areas studied during the 1950s.

Saini[37] studied the relationship between farm size and farm business income per farm, using Farm Management Studies data pertaining to the mid-'50s and mid-'60s. He estimated two regression equations of the form:

$$\log Q = \log A + \alpha \log X; \text{ and}$$
$$\log Y = \log C + \beta \log X.$$

where,

Q = gross value of output per farm;
Y = far business income per farm; and
X = farm size.

These two equations were separately estimated for Uttar Pradesh and Punjab. He also studied the disparities in farm income arising from Green Revolution.

His study showed that there was inverse relationship between farm size and income per acre in both the regions, during the mid-'50s. This relationship, according to Saini, had undergone a significant change after the setting-in of the Green Revolution. The important finding of this paper is that the inverse relationship yielded place to a positive relationship in the post-Green Revolution period. The study indicated that as farm size increased, income increased more than proportionately. This result was sufficient to argue that the income gap between small and large farms had widened after the setting-in of the Green Revolution. He further argued on the basis of his result that there had been growing inequalities in household incomes which were further aggravated by the differences in factor endowments and resources of the different size classes of farms. He concluded that the big farmers had gained considerably from the new technology.

The inequalities in income distribution from high-yielding varieties rice was examined by Kalirajan[38] in the context of Seyyampalayam village in Coimbatore district. About 91 farmers cultivating high-yielding varieties rice in both kharif and rabi 1977-78 were selected, using stratified random sampling method. There were 50 small and 41 large farmers. The concentration of net profits among the participants in the two seasons was examined by using Gini coefficient. The distribution pattern of net profits (total revenue less total variable cost, i.e., farm residual income) was similar for both farmer groups in the two seasons. The analysis revealed that there was considerable inequality in income distribution in them. However, the inequality was greater in rabi than in kharif.

The following three factors were considered in analysing the reasons for inequality of gains : (i) unequal distribution of ownership of operational holding, (ii) unequal distribution of input application per acre between farm size groups, and (iii) different yield responses from same level of input application per acre between operational holdings. He found that the crucial factor determining the distribution of net profits was the pattern of land ownership in both seasons. This suggests that government has to rely heavily on policy measures in relation to land reforms. He concluded that the gains from High Yielding Varieties Programme were enjoyed equally by farms of all size groups.

3.4 Economic Efficiency

Economic efficiency is the most important tool for the evaluation of decision-making in the production process. It measures the results of an objective, in relation to the efforts made. The efforts in agriculture relate to the allocation of scarce resources among alternative uses to maximise profits. Decision-making of a farmer relates to his ability and aim to achieve the maximum possible output with a given set of inputs.

Economic efficiency comprises technical efficiency and price efficiency. It measures the cost-price relationship between input and output. Technical efficiency measures a farmer's ability of obtaining the maximum output from a given set of inputs. It deals with the management of production factors. Price efficiency measures the ability of a farmer in equating marginal value product with marginal cost of the inputs. It deals with the achievement of maximum profits from varying factor proportions and improving market imperfections.

The literature provides three methods of measuring the production efficiency of farmers.[39] They are: (i) single-factor productivity estimates, (ii) conventional production function, and (iii) the profit function approach. However, the choice of a particular measure of efficiency depends upon the objective of the study.

(i) *Single-factor productivity estimates*

It measures a farmer's production behaviour relating to the returns to a single factor of production (like labour, capital, land, etc.) valued at market price. This measure is a partial measure of efficiency. However, the assumption of market price of a factor being same for all producers may not exist in practice. Further, the optimum level of production is not specified by the approach. This makes comparisons of these measures difficult.

(ii) *Production function analysis*

It is widely used in measuring the production efficiencies of farmers owning different sizes of operational holdings. The analysis neither incorporates prices as exogenous variables nor allows for imperfect maximisation. The basic assumption of the production function is that output alone is subject to random errors. When the marginal value product is equated to its marginal cost, it has the consequence that all inputs are likely to be subject to random efforts. Therefore, this contradicts the assumption that only output is subject to random errors.

Theoretically, all farmers may produce identical output using identical inputs, provided they have the same production functions, face the same input and output prices and maximise profits. However, this kind of situation may not prevail in practice. Even if all farms are profit maximisers, they produce the same output using different factor intensities and face different fixed factors like land, technical knowledge, socio-economic conditions, etc. These variations in prices and fixed factors of production contribute to different degrees of price and technical efficiency, resulting in different overall economic efficiency among farms.

(iii) *The profit function approach*

A profit function can well-explain the production behaviour of farmers, as it incorporates prices as explaining variables and allows for imperfect profit maximisation by the farmers. It also allows for the payment and receipts of different prices for homogenous variable inputs and output, respectively, and for varying quantities of fixed inputs. Thus, it takes care of the inter-farm variations in equating marginal value of product with the prices of variable inputs. It also has the benefit of incorporating technical and price efficiency components of economic efficiency, unlike the production function.

Using the duality between production and cost functions, Lau and Yotopoulos[40] derived unit output price (UOP) profit function and factor demand functions. They developed an approach to isolate the technical and price efficiency components between small and large farmer groups. The equations adopted for estimating UOP profit function and factor demand functions were of the form:

$$\log \pi = \log A_*^S + \delta_L^* D_L + \sum_{(i=1)}^{4} \delta_i^* D_i + \alpha_1^* \log W$$

$$+ \beta_1^* \log K + \beta_2^* \log T$$

and $$\frac{-WL}{\pi} = \alpha_1^{*L} D_L + \alpha_1^{*S} D_S$$

where,

π = farm profit (total revenue minus variable cost) in money terms,

L = labour in man-hours,

W = money wage rate,

D_L = dummy for large farmer,

D_S = dummy for small farmer,

D_i = dummy for states,

K = fixed factors representing interest on fixed capital, and

T = cultivated area.

The methodology used for testing the differences in different relative efficiency were:

(a) *Test for equal relative economic efficiency*

$$H_0 : \delta_L^* = 0$$

The hypotheses to be tested is the existence of equal relative economic efficiency among small farmers and large farmers. For this, the UOP profit functions and variable factor demand functions of large and small farmer groups should coincide with each other. In other words, the dummy variable coefficient δ_L^* should equal zero. If the hypothesis is rejected, it may be inferred that economic efficiency differs for the two farmer groups.

(b) *Test for equal relative price efficiency*

$$H_0 : \alpha_1^{*L} = \alpha_1^{*S}$$

The hypotheses tests whether small and large farms equate marginal value product to marginal cost to the same degree. It tests whether the elasticities of variable inputs estimated from factor demand functions are the same for small (α_1^{*S}) and large (α_1^{*L}) farmers. If the null hypothesis is rejected, it implies that small and large farmers do not maximise profits to the same degree.

(c) *Test for equal relative technical and price efficiency*

$$H_0 : \delta_L^* = 0, \qquad \text{and} \qquad \alpha_1^{*S} = \alpha_1^{*L}$$

The hypothesis of technical efficiency consists of jointly testing the equality between economic and price efficiencies. If the null hypothesis is accepted, it indicates that the two groups of farmers are equal in technical and price efficiency. If hypothesis (a) is rejected, then the rejection of hypothesis (c) may also be expected.

(d) *Test for absolute price efficiency of small and large farmers*

$$H_0 : \alpha_1^{*S} = \alpha_1^{*} \quad ; \text{and}$$

$$\alpha_1^{*L} = \alpha_1^{*}$$

The hypotheses test whether the farmers (large and small) maximise their profits, by equating their respective marginal value product to marginal cost. For this, the elasticities of variable inputs (α_1^{*t} and α_1^{*L}) computed from the factor demand function should equal their respective profit function elasticities (α_1^{*}). If the hypotheses are rejected, it may be inferred that the individual farmer groups do not maximise their profits.

Using the Cobb-Douglas form of profit function, output supply and input demand elasticities, own and cross price elasticities of demand for variable inputs and direct and indirect estimates can be studied along with economic efficiency of farmer groups. Given below are the main findings of a few related studies for India and other countries. It would give an insight into the behaviour of the above-stated aspects, using different combinations of factors of production under different environmental conditions.

Lau and Yotopoulos[41] specified Cobb-Douglas form of profit function and empirically formulated the test of relative economic efficiency. A crucial feature of the profit function analysis is that it assumes that farms behave according to certain decision rules (which include the profit maximisation rules), given the prices of output and variable inputs and the quantities of their fixed factors of production. A comparison of relative efficiency of two groups of farms was made under the approach by examining the coefficient of the group dummy variable. Farm Management Studies data were used to test equal economic efficiency of small and large farms. About 2,962 holdings were selected from six Indian states, covering a three-year period, 1955-57.

The test of relative economic efficiency was in favour of small farms. It appeared that, given the fixed factors of production (land and fixed capital) and within the ranges of the observed prices of output and variable inputs, small farms had higher actual profits. This implied that they attained higher levels of price efficiency and/or technical efficiency. This suggested that the supervisory role of the owner-manager of the farm may be crucial for attaining high levels of economic efficiency. However, the source of difference in economic efficiency between the small and large farmers was not identified in the study.

Using the same Farm Management Studies data used in the 1971 study, Yotopoulos and Lau[42] analysed the relative economic efficiency between small and large farms, with the object of identifying and isolating the causes for difference in the economic efficiency of the two farm groups. In the analysis, they further developed an operational model to separately measure relative technical and price efficiency between farm groups.

The results revealed that small farms were relatively economically more efficient than large farms. They earned higher actual profits than the latter. However, the relative economic efficiency of small farms was not due to superior price efficiency. In fact, both the farm groups were found to be price efficient. The difference was due to the superior technical efficiency of small farms. During the study period, constant returns to scale was identified in Indian agriculture. Hence, consolidation of small farms on the grounds of economies of scale was not favoured.

Using the cross-section data for 1967 and 1968 from official sources, Lau, Lin and Yotopoulos[43] estimated the short-run output supply and factor demand function for paddy cultivation in Taiwan agriculture. About 400 farm households grouped according to five sizes of operation and eight agricultural regions were studied. The framework of Cobb-Douglas normalized restricted profit function along with four variable inputs (labour, mechanical input, animal input and fertilizer) and two fixed inputs (land and capital assets) were jointly estimated.

The hypotheses of profit maximisation and constant returns to scale and structural change were tested and confirmed. The own price elasticities of output and variable inputs were all greater than one in absolute terms. The cross price elasticities between the variable inputs indicated that they were all complements rather than substitutes. The output supply and factor demand were highly sensitive to changes in output price, especially the latter.

Striking differences in the direct and indirect estimates of the same parameter were observed. The direct estimates of the production elasticities for land and labour were very low due to simultaneous equations bias. In the indirect estimates, labour and land were the two most important factor inputs, followed by fertilizer. Other inputs did not figure prominently. The importance of labour input showed that despite substantial technological progress in Taiwan agriculture, most of the innovations had been labour-intensive in nature.

Adulavidhaya, et al,[44] estimated a short-run output supply and factor demand function for a sample of rice farmers in Thailand. The profit function approach was used with four variable inputs (labour, animal input, mechanical input and seed fertilizers) and two fixed inputs (fixed farm assets and farm size). Data were collected from six provinces in the Central Plain and North East of Thailand for the crop year 1972 to March 1973.

The hypotheses of profit maximisation and constant returns to scale were tested and confirmed. Output supply and factor demands were highly sensitive to changes in output price. The own price elasticities of output and variable inputs indicated an elastic response of factor utilisation. The cross price elasticities between all variable inputs (except, output and labour) indicated that these inputs were complements rather than substitutes. The indirect estimates of production function were reasonable and emphasized the importance of labour in Thailand agriculture. Land and fixed assets were the next most important factors of production.

Flinn, Kalirajan and Castillo[45] estimated rice supply and input demand elasticities, using profit function analysis, for a sample of 81 rice farmers in Laguna, Philippines. Data were collected from farmers using advanced methods of irrigated rice culture during the wet season, 1978. The variables used were fertilizer, pesticides, mechanical power, animal power, labour for transplanting, labour for crop maintenance, rice area and capital service flow.

The analysis showed that given the technology and resources at their disposal, the sample farmers maximised their short-run profits with respect to normalized prices of the variable inputs. The farmers responded to price changes in an efficient manner. Output supply was highly responsive to rice price. On the input side, output supply was most sensitive to wage rates and cost of mechanical land preparation and to a lesser extent to fertilizer. The elasticity of rice output with respect to land (0.7) and capital (0.1) indicated that farm size had a substantial impact on farm profits when compared to increase in capital intensity per farm.

The direct and indirect production elasticities implied the prevalence of decreasing returns to scale. The production elasticities estimated for land were 0.36 and 0.38 respectively. The indirect estimate for fertilizer was higher than for pesticides. This was reasonable, as the Laguna farmers grew modern varieties which were both fertilizer-responsive and resistant to many of the common rice pests.

The unique feature of the paper is that the authors justified the use of profit function methodology by reporting the coefficient of variation for the price data, which ranged from nine to 28 per cent. They argued that qualitative differences were unlikely to be important sources of measured price variation for rice and fertilizer, as they are fairly standard products. Further, they indicated that price difference may be attributed to transport cost and variations in dealer prices.

Dutta[46] judged the relative efficiency of small versus large farms and peasant versus capitalist farms, using Lau-Yotopoulos profit function model. The analysis was based on the data collected in the agricultural year 1977-78, from a sample of 150 agricultural households, randomly selected and stratified for different classes of holdings. Paddy and wheat crops in Ranchi district were chosen for the study. However, only the findings relating to rice cultivation are outlined here.

The analysis showed that small farms were relatively more

efficient with regard to paddy cultivation. The coefficient of dummy variable for large farms turned out to be significantly negative. The lower intercept term for large farms suggested their lower level of economic efficiency. The statistical tests with regard to the differences in the profit function for peasant and capitalist groups of farm indicated that the former were relatively more efficient than the latter. This suggested that the role of peasant proprietorship is significant in the cultivation of crops. Family labour contributes greater care and attention when compared to hired labour in the raising of crops. Since the study was based on single-equation model, Dutta did not identify the source of differences in economic efficiency.

Junankar[47] tested the joint hypotheses of profit maximisation behaviour and competitive behaviour, using Cobb-Douglas profit function along with input demand equations. Farm Management Studies data were used for Tanjore district of Tamil Nadu, for the year 1969-70. The study was confined to rice crops, as the district is relatively prosperous in the cultivation of high-yielding varieties of paddy. The analysis revealed that Indian farmers were not profit maximisers under competitive conditions. He explained that both small and large farmers did not operate in the same market. He pointed out that more research needed to be done along these lines to explain the behaviour of farmers in poor countries.

Tamin[48] studied the output supply and factor demand functions for Malaysian paddy farming. He adopted the Cobb-Douglas form of normalised restricted profit function with four variable inputs (labour, animal input, mechanical input and fertilizers) and fixed inputs (land and fixed assets) for the analysis. Data were obtained from a cross-sectional survey in MUDA Irrigation Region conducted in February and April 1973. A three-stage sampling procedure was adopted.

The farmers were profit maximisers. Constant returns to scale was found to exist. A 10 per cent increase in price of output could increase output supply only by a little over 4.17 per cent, indicating that output supply was inelastic to output price. Among variable inputs, a 10 per cent decrease in labour wage rate resulted in a 25 per cent increase in the output supply. The response of output supply with respect to fertilizer was quite low (–0.8). On the basis of this result, the author argued that fertilizer subsidy programme would not be effective in raising output supply in the study area, whatever its effect on income distribution.

The impact of output price on the demand for variable inputs was very strong. More specifically, a 10 per cent increase in the price of output could result in a 14 per cent increase in the demand for variable inputs. The demand elasticities were negative with respect to own price and positive in response to the prices of output and fixed inputs. The negative signs of the cross price elasticities revealed that the variable factors were complements. The indirect estimates revealed the dominance of land (0.654) as the most important source of productivity, followed by labour (0.180).

The relative economic efficiency between owner farm and tenant farm households and small and large farms were studied separately. The result indicated no significant difference in the relative technical and price efficiencies of owner farms and tenant farms. This applied to both large and small farmers also. The results implied that no form of farm organisation could be preferred based on efficiency considerations.

Using Lau-Yotopoulos profit function, Kalirajan[49] examined the economic efficiency of farmers growing IR 20 rice in rabi (winter) season of 1977-78. A random sample of 70 farmers were selected from Seyyampalayam village of Coimbatore district. Equal representation was given to small and large farmer groups (35 each) in the sample. The independent variables used in the analysis were labour, fertilizer, pesticides, bullock pair, land and capital flows.

The study showed the prevalence of equal relative economic efficiency in rice cultivation among the two farmer groups. Equal price and technical efficiency also existed between them. The test of full profit maximisation revealed that the two groups did not perfectly maximise their profits. This indicated that they did not make optimal utilisation of the variable factors. The analysis implied that both the farmer groups were not able to equate marginal value product and marginal cost for pesticides, despite using the recommended doses of the input. Based on this result, the author argued that this was due to the biological characteristics of the variety, the maturity period of which does not enable pesticides to work effectively on the BPH pest. Thus according to him, the local pest was the disturbing factor affecting decision-making of the sample farmers.

An overall glance at the literatures reviewed here clearly indicates that agriculture has undergone tremendous change during the new technological era at global level. The review on cost of cultivation reveals that there is a considerable increase in the cost of cultivation in favour of the modern inputs. A survey of the works on yield gap shows that this phenomenon is the product of environmental constraints between the experimental station and farms, while between the best farm and average farm, it mainly arises out of the biological and socio-economic constraints. Studies on farm size and productivity at different points of time and in different regions indicate that no definite relationship between the two has been established so far. Thus, the subject of farm size and productivity still remains a controversial issue to be further probed into. Literatures on economic efficiency reviewed here are based on Cobb-Douglas profit function. The major findings of these studies indicate that economic efficiency of small versus large farms and tenant versus owner farms is also a still-debated issue, requiring more enquiries into the aspect.

NOTES

1. A.S. Kahlon and Karam Singh, "Farm Efficiency Measures", *Economics of Farm Management in India: Theory and Practice*, Allied Publishers Pvt. Ltd., New Delhi, 1981, pp. 75-103.
2. V. Rajagopalan, et al., *Studies on Cost of Production of Major Crops in Tamil Nadu*, Department of Agricultural Economics, Tamil Nadu Agricultural University, Coimbatore, 1978, pp. 2-3.
3. Hanumantha Rao, "Changes in Costs and Returns with the Use of High Yielding Seeds", *Technological Change and Distribution of Gains in Indian Agriculture*, Macmillan Company of India Ltd., Delhi, 1975, pp. 75-88.
4. Rajagopalan, et al., op. cit.
5. J.P. Singh and K.V. Govindaraju, "New Technology of Paddy Yield: Adoption and Yield Differentials", *New Seeds: Adoption and Yield*, Sterling Publishers Pvt. Ltd., New Delhi, 1979, pp. 3-89.
6. Madhusudan Ghosh, "Farm Size Productivity Nexus under an Alternative Technology", *Indian Journal of Agricultural Economics*, Vol. 41, No. 1, January-March 1986, pp. 17-28.
7. James Quigley Harrison, Agricultural Modernization and Income Distribution: An Economic Analysis of the Impact of New Seed Varieties on the Crop Production of Large and Small Farms in India, (mimeo), Ph.D., Princeton University, 1972.
8. K. Kalirajan, "The Contribution of Location Specific Research to Agricultural Productivity", *Indian Journal of Agricultural Economics*, Vol. 35, No. 4, October-December 1980, pp. 8-16.
9. Akimi Fujimoto, "Farm Management Analysis of Malay and Chinese Rice Farming in Province of Wellesley, Malaysia", *Journal of Developing Economies*, Vol. XXI, No. 1, March 1983, pp. 35-50.
10. M.S. Swaminathan, Lecture, *The Hindu*, 19th March, 1983, in "Bridging Gap in

Yields between Average Farms and Research Centres", *Monthly Reporter*, Vol. 9, No. 5, Director of Agriculture, Madras, October 1983, p.1.
11. Kwanchi A. Gomez, "On-Farm Assessment of Yield Constraints: Methodological Problems", *Constraints to High Yields on Asian Rice Farms: An Interim Report*, International Rice Research Institute, Philippines, October 1977, pp. 1-16.
12. Randolph Barker, "Adoption and Production Impact of New Rice Technology: The Yield Constraints Problems", *Farm-Level Constraints to High Rice Yields in Asia, 1974-'77*, IRRI, Philippines, 1979, pp. 1-26.
13. Gomez, loc. cit.
14. J.C. Flinn and Mubarak Ali, "Technical Efficiency in Basmati Rice Production", *Pakistan Journal of Applied Economics*, Vol. 5, No. 1, 1986, pp. 1-22.
15. D.K. Mukherji, *Gap Analysis—An Effective Production Increase Concept in Rice*, Summary of Lecture delivered at the State Level Training Meeting on Rice held at Purila, Department of Agriculture, West Bengal, India, July 1977.
16. Flinn and Ali, loc. cit.
17. B.R. Davidson and B.R. Martin, "The Relationship between Yields on Farms and in Experiments", *Australian Journal of Agricultural Economics*, Vol. 9, No. 2, December 1965, pp. 129-140.
18. A.N. Sadhu and R.K. Mahajan, "Resource Use Efficiency and New Agricultural Technology", *Technological Change and Agricultural Development in India*, Himalaya Publishing House, Delhi, 1985, pp. 135-174.
19. G.R. Saini, "Allocation Efficiency in Agriculture—Crop Level Analysis", *Farm Size, Resource Use Efficiency and Income Distribution*, Allied Publishers Pvt. Ltd., New Delhi, 1979, pp. 74-89.
20. K. Kalirajan and R.T. Shand, "Location Specific Research: Rice Technology in India", *Land Economics*, Vol. 58, No. 4, November 1982, pp. 537-546.
21. Kamphel Adulavidhaya, et al., "Rice Production and Development in Thailand", *Constraints of High Yields on Asian Rice Farms: An Interim Report*, IRRI, Philippines, October 1977, pp. 203-235.
22. Yi-Chung Kuo, Carson Wu and Cheng Chang Li, "Rice Production in Taiwan's Agriculture", Ibid., pp. 177-201.
23. S.K. De Datta and others, "Constraints to High Rice Yields, Nueva Ecija, Philippines", *Farm-Level Constraints to High Rice Yields in Asia: 1974-77*, IRRI, Philippines, 1979, pp. 191-234.
24. Carson Wu, Yi-Chung Kuo and Cheng Chang Li, "Agro-economic Study of Rice Production in Taiwan", Ibid., pp. 349-393.
25. Fujimoto, loc. cit.
26. A.M. Khusro, "Returns to Scale in Indian Agriculture", *Indian Journal of Agricultural Economics*, Vol. XIX, Nos. 3&4, July-December 1964, p.51.
27. Ibid., p.52.
28. Hanumantha Rao, "Farm Size and the Distribution of Gains", op.cit., pp. 136-150.
29. Khusro, op. cit., pp. 51-80.
30. Raj Krishna, "Some Production Function for the Punjab", *Indian Journal of Agricultural Economics*, Vol. XIX, Nos. 3&4, July-December 1964, pp. 87-97.
31. Hanumantha Rao, loc. cit.
32. Raj Krishna, loc. cit.
33. M. Chattopadhyay and Ashok Rudra, "Size-Productivity Revisited", *Economic*

and Political Weekly, Review of Agriculture, Vol. XI, No. 39, September 25, 1976, pp. A-104–A-116.

34. Manabendu Chattopadhyay and Ashok Rudra, "Size-Productivity Revisited", *Economic and Political Weekly*, Vol. XII, No. 11, March 12, 1977, pp. 476-484.
35. Ashok Rudra and Amartya Sen, "Farm Size and Labour Use: Analysis and Policy", *Economic and Political Weekly*, Annual No. , Vol. XV, Nos. 5,6&7, February 1980, pp. 391-394.
36. Khusro, loc. cit.
37. G.R. Saini, "Green Revolution and Disparities in Farm Income – A Comment", *Economic and Political Weekly*, Vol. XI, No. 26, November 13, 1976, pp. 1804-1806.
38. K. Kalirajan, "Benefits from the High-Yielding Varieties Programme and their Distribution in an Irrigated Paddy Area", *Indian Journal of Agricultural Economics*, Vol. 35, No. 3, July-September 1980, pp. 70-76.
39. K. Kalirajan, "Testing the Hypothesis of Equal Relative Economic Efficiency Using Restricted Aitken's Least Squares Estimation", *Journal of Development Studies*, Vol. 17, No. 4, July 1981, p.308.
40. P.A. Yotopoulos and L.J. Lau, "A Test for Relative Economic Efficiency – Some Further Results", *American Economic Review*, Vol. 63, No. 3, 1973, pp. 214-23.
41. L.J. Lau and P.A. Yotopoulos, "A Test for Relative Efficiency and Application to Indian Agriculture", *American Economic Review*, Vol. 61, March 1971, pp. 94-109.
42. Yotopoulos and Lau, loc. cit.
43. L.J. Lau, Wuu-Long Lin and P.A. Yotopoulos, "Efficiency and Technological Change in Taiwan's Agriculture", *Resource Use in Agriculture: Application of the Profit Function to Selected Countries*, (Ed.) P.A. Yotopoulos and L.J. Lau, Food Research Institute Studies, Vol. XVII, No. 1, 1979, pp. 23-50.
44. Kamphel Adulavidhaya, et al., "A Micro Economic Analysis of the Agriculture of Thailand", Ibid., pp. 79-86.
45. J.C. Flinn, K. Kalirajan and Linda L. Castillo, "Supply Responsiveness of Rice Farmers in Laguna, Philippines", *Australian Journal of Agricultural Economics*, Vol. 26, No. 1, April 1982, pp. 39-48.
46. L.N. Dutta, "Relative Efficiency, Farm Size and Peasant Proprietorship – A Case Study of Ranchi District (Bihar)", *Indian Journal of Agricultural Economics*, Vol. 37, No. 1, January-March 1982, pp. 76-82.
47. P.N. Junankar, "Do Indian Farmers Maximise Profits?", *Journal of Development Studies*, Vol. 17, No. 1, October 1980, pp. 48-61.
48. Mokhtar Tamin, "Micro Economic Analysis of Production Behaviour of Malaysian Farms: Lessons from MUDA", (Eds.) Yotopoulos and Lau, op.cit., pp. 87-98.
49. K. Kalirajan, "The Economic Efficiency of Farmers Growing High-Yielding, Irrigated Rice in India", *American Journal of Agricultural Economics*, Vol. 63, No. 3, August 1981, pp. 566-570.

4

COST AND RETURN STRUCTURE

It is widely accepted that the adoption of New Agricultural Technology (NAT) not only promises a greater output but also entails a higher cost of cultivation. This chapter provides an insight into the cost and return structure of farmers growing IR 20 and CO 37 rice varieties and of small and large farmer groups cultivating IR 20 variety, during the rabi season of 1985-86 in Gokilapuram village. The chapter also highlights their input-output structure and requirements of hired labour for the various farm activities involved in rice cultivation. Besides, in the light of their comparative cost of production and profits earned, the economics of producing the two varieties is also discussed in the chapter.

4.1 **Input-Output Structure**

The input-output structure per acre of IR 20 and CO 37 varieties of rice is presented in Table 4.1.

It may be observed that while the producers of IR 20 variety obtained an output of 2,367.35 kg, CO 37 variety yielded only 2,248.60 kg per acre. It projects a significant difference of 118.75 kg per acre between the yields of the two varieties.

The average requirements of human labour for IR 20 cultivation was about 120 mandays per acre. Likewise, for CO 37 variety it was nearly 124 mandays. Bullock labour used per acre was almost the same (i.e., about nine pairs each) for the two varieties.

The application of chemical fertilizers differed significantly by 36.19 kg between the two varieties. The quantity of fertilizer required for IR 20 variety (195.48 kg) turned out to be greater than its requirement for CO 37 (159.29 kg). This may be due to the greater responsiveness of IR 20 variety to fertilizer compared to CO 37 rice.[1] The pesticide requirements of the two varieties worked out to be around nine kg each. The amount spent on seeds sown per acre by the producers of the two rice varieties did not exhibit much variations. On an average, Rs. 117.50 and Rs. 114.40 worth of seeds per acre were respectively required for IR and CO 37 rice cultivation.

TABLE 4.1: Input and Output Structure per acre of IR 20 and CO 37 Rice Varieties, Rabi 1985-86

Particulars	Unit	IR 20	CO 37	*t*-Value (IR 20 vs CO 37)
1. Seeds	Rs.	117.50 (22.50)	114.40 (21.76)	0.81
2. Bullock Labour	Pairs	8.93 (1.72)	8.80 (1.33)	0.52
3. Human Labour	Mandays	120.24 (26.96)	123.66 (15.38)	1.22
4. Chemical Fertilizer	kg.	195.48 (44.75)	159.29 (46.01)	4.58*
5. Pesticides	kg.	9.15 (5.69)	8.49 (1.90)	1.05
6. Yield	kg.	2367.35 (235.03)	2248.60 (237.98)	2.89*
Sample Size		100	50	

Note: Figures in parentheses represent standard deviation.
* Indicates significance at 5 per cent level.

Thus, the analysis showed an evidence of a definite superiority of IR 20 over CO 37 in terms of the average yield acquired per acre. This is contradictory to the findings of Kalirajan and Shand[2] who found the location-specific varieties (ADT 31 and CO 37) to be superior than the exotic variety (IR 20) in Coimbatore district. The levels of variable inputs used per acre revealed that the use of fertilizer differed significantly between the two varieties. However, the use of other inputs for IR 20 and CO 37 rice cultivation was almost similar.

Table 4.1.1 illustrates the average input use and output obtained on small and large farms growing IR 20 variety of rice.

On an average, the small farmers reaped a yield of 2,422.01 kg while the large farmers received 2,213.69 kg per acre. There was a significant surplus of 208.32 kg in the yield per acre realised by small farmers compared to the large farmers cultivating IR 20 rice.

TABLE 4.1.1: Input and Output Structure per acre of IR 20 Farmer Groups, Rabi 1985-86

Particulars	Unit	IR 20 Rice		t-Value (S.F.vs L.F.)
		Small Farmers	Large Farmers	
1. Seeds	Rs.	117.37 (20.71)	117.86 (26.94)	0.08
2. Bullock Labour	Pairs	9.28 (1.77)	7.88 (1.07)	4.78*
3. Human Labour	Mandays	123.32 (27.47)	111.46 (23.79)	2.10*
4. Chemical Fertilizer	kg	198.80 (48.53)	186.07 (33.74)	1.46
5. Pesticides	kg	10.63 (5.41)	4.91 (4.18)	5.54*
6. Yield	kg	2422.01 (232.09)	2213.69 (164.46)	4.95*
Sample Size		74	26	

Note: Figures in parentheses represent standard deviation.
S.F. = Small Farmers; and L.F. = Large Farmers.
* Indicates significance at 5 per cent level.

The average number of mandays employed by small farmers was about 123 per acre, while it was nearly 111 mandays in the case of large farmers. A more intensive use of family labour by the former accounts for most of this difference. The number of bullock pairs used by the small farmers and large farmers was around nine and eight, respectively. The ownership of bullock pair by small farmers enable them to use the input as much as required. The difference in employment of human and animal labour inputs per acre emerged statistically significant between the two farmer groups.

Small farmers applied 198.80 kg and large farmers, 186.07 kg of chemical fertilizer per acre. The latter group used only about half the quantity of pesticides (4.91 kg) used per acre by the former group (10.63 kg). Small farmers made greater use of the input, as a protection against pest-attack and to ensure a good yield. The amount spent on the quantity of seeds sown per acre by the two sets of farmers was almost identical.

In sum, levels of input application were greater on small farms compared to large farms. The use of human labour, bullock labour and pesticides differed significantly between the two classes of farmers. The more intensive use of inputs by small farmers could be because most of the crop is produced for domestic consumption by them. The yield obtained was also larger on small farms. Besides the greater input use by small farmers, it may be attributed to the better supervision and farm management made possible by the smaller size of their operational holdings. Subramaniyan,[3] Harrison[4] and Singh and Govindaraju[5] arrived at similar conclusions.

4.2 Labour Requirements

This section of the chapter provides details on the number and cost of employing male and female labour for IR 20 and CO 37 farming by their producers. The farm activities involved in rice cultivation were broadly classified under eight heads, viz., (1) preparatory cultivation, (2) sowing and transplantation, (3) application of organic manure and inorganic fertilizers, (4) plant protection measures, (5) weeding, (6) irrigation , (7) harvesting, and (8) threshing.

The average number of male and female labour employed and the expenditure incurred on them for IR 20 and CO 37 rice cultivation are presented in Table 4.2.

TABLE 4.2: Average Requirements of Hired Labour per acre for Various Farm Activities in Rice Cultivation, Rabi 1985-86

Farm Activities	IR 20 Rice				
	M.L.	F.L.	M.L.C.	F.L.C.	T.L.C.
1. Preparatory Cultivation	9.1	–	127.41	–	127.41
2. Sowing and Transplantation	–	19.53	–	198.94	198.94
3. Application of Organic Manure and Inorganic Fertilizers	0.38	0.77	5.44	4.69	10.13
4. Plant Protection Measures	1.55	–	21.58	–	21.58
5. Weeding	–	35.76	–	212.24	212.24
6. Irrigation	8.17	–	124.90	–	124.90
7. Harvesting	–	22.88	–	266.25	266.25
8. Threshing	3.46	5.27	47.34	50.03	97.37
Total	23.20	84.21	326.67	732.15	1058.82

TABLE 4.2 *(Contd.)*

Farm Activities	CO 37 Rice				
	M.L.	F.L.	M.L.C.	F.L.C.	T.L.C.
1. Preparatory Cultivation	9.58	–	131.19	–	131.19
2. Sowing and Transplantation	–	19.78	–	205.83	205.83
3. Application of Organic Manure and Inorganic Fertilizers	0.28	0.74	4.10	4.41	8.51
4. Plant Protection Measures	1.44	–	17.97	–	17.97
5. Weeding	–	39.96	–	237.10	237.10
6. Irrigation	9.06	–	121.93	–	121.93
7. Harvesting	–	22.14	–	290.22	290.22
8. Threshing	3.42	4.44	50.92	45.44	96.36
Total	23.78	87.06	326.11	783.00	1109.11

Note: M.L. = Number of Male Labour Employed;
F.L. = Number of Female Labour Employed;
M.L.C. = Male Labour Cost;
F.L.C. = Female Labour Cost; and
T.L.C. = Total Labour Cost.

The IR 20 growers incurred a total labour cost of Rs. 1,058.82 on about 107 hired labourers, constituting 23 males and 84 females. At the same time, the producers of CO 37 rice incurred a total labour cost of Rs. 1,109.11 per acre on employment of 111 labourers (i.e., 24 males and 87 females). Apparently, the cultivators of the latter variety employed relatively more number of labourers at a higher labour cost than the former for the various farm activities of rice cultivation, during the season.

Rice cultivation in general was observed to be quite labour intensive in Gokilapuram. The composition of male and female labour employment was almost similar for the two rice cultivation. Female labour was preferred for nearly all farm activities, except preparatory cultivation, plant protection measures and irrigation. The maximum number of labourers were employed in activities of weeding, harvesting and sowing and transplantation. Incidently, only female workers were preferred for these works. Unnevehr and Stanford[6] confirmed this result in their study on women labour in

Asian rice farming. Studies of Subramaniyan[7] and Aiyasamy, Rajagopalan and Sundaresan[8] also supported this finding.

Female labourers were paid relatively lower wages than their male counterparts, for similar labour performed. On an average, a female worker engaged in IR 20 cultivation received Rs. 8.69, while a male worker earned Rs. 14.08 per day. The respective average wages paid per day were Rs. 8.99 and Rs. 13.71, in the case of CO 37 cultivation. The employment of a greater number of women in farming could be due to the nature of work and the comparative cheapness of female labour in the labour market.

In brief, the CO 37 farmers employed more labourers at a higher labour cost compared to the cultivators of IR 20 variety. Rice farming was labour-intensive in the study area. The pattern of labour employment for the two rice cultivation was almost similar. Female labour was preferred to male labour for most of the farm activities. This could be due to the nature of agricultural work and their relative cheapness in terms of wage payments.

Table 4.2.1 gives comparative information on the average number of male and female labourers employed per acre and the wage paid to them by the small and large farmer groups engaged in IR 20 rice cultivation.

TABLE 4.2.1: Average Requirements of Hired Labour per acre for Various Farm Activities by IR 20 Farmer Groups, Rabi 1985-86

Farm Activities	Small Farmers				
	M.L.	F.L.	M.L.C.	F.L.C.	T.L.C.
1. Preparatory Cultivation	9.38	–	132.77	–	132.77
2. Sowing and Transplantation	–	19.35	–	195.99	195.99
3. Application of Organic Manure and Inorganic Fertilizers	0.35	0.77	4.92	4.71	9.63
4. Plant Protection Measures	1.72	–	24.04	–	24.04
5. Weeding	–	35.34	–	211.44	211.44
6. Irrigation	8.77	–	123.10	–	123.10
7. Harvesting	–	23.69	–	275.09	275.09
8. Threshing	3.64	5.51	49.86	52.24	102.10
Total	23.86	84.66	334.69	739.47	1074.16

TABLE 4.2.1 (*Contd.*)

Farm Activities	Large Farmers				
	M.L.	F.L.	M.L.C.	F.L.C.	T.L.C.
1. Preparatory Cultivation	8.31	–	112.18	–	112.18
2. Sowing and Transplantation	–	20.04	–	207.34	207.34
3. Application of Organic Manure and Inorganic Fertilizers	0.46	0.77	6.92	4.61	11.53
4. Plant Protection Measures	1.08	–	14.57	–	14.57
5. Weeding	–	36.96	–	214.52	214.52
6. Irrigation	8.54	–	130.06	–	130.06
7. Harvesting	–	20.58	–	241.11	241.11
8. Threshing	2.96	4.58	40.17	64.36	104.53
Total	21.35	82.93	303.90	731.94	1035.84

The result shows that the expenses on total labour employed for the various farm activities were higher on small farms. The total labour cost per acre worked out to be Rs. 1,074.16 for small farmers and Rs. 1,035.84 for large farmers during the season. The average number of labourers engaged by the former was about 24 females and 85 females, while the latter employed nearly 21 and 83 labourers respectively.

The composition of male and female labour was almost identical for the two sets of farmers. Female labourers were preferred for most of the farm activities. This trend is observed to be traditionally prevalent in India in particular and Asian rice farming in general.[9] Weeding, harvesting and sowing and transplantation were the activities requiring most of the labour employed.

Women labourers were paid relatively lower wages than the men. Small farmers paid Rs. 8.73 and Rs. 14.03 respectively, while the large farmers paid them Rs. 8.83 and Rs. 14.23. However, not much difference was noticed in the wage payments made by the two farmer groups.

To conclude, small farmers incurred greater expenses on labour employment compared to the large farmers. The composition of labour employment was similar for the two groups. Most of the farm activities were performed by women workers. They were also paid lower wages than the men. The nature of agricultural work and the relative cheapness of women labour explain their greater employment in farming. These findings are similar to the results of Subramaniyan.[10]

4.3 Cost and Return Structure

The average cost and return structure of IR 20 and CO 37 varieties of rice are depicted in Table 4.3.

TABLE 4.3: Cost and Return Structure per acre of IR 20 and CO 37 Varieties of Rice, Rabi 1985-86

Cost Components	IR 20 Total Farmers		CO 37 Total Farmers		t-value (IR 20 vs. CO 37)
	Value in Rs.	%	Value in Rs.	%	
(i) Human Labour (including Family Labour)	1225.85 (242.47)	37.28	1251.09 (182.46)	39.89	0.71
(ii) Bullock Labour	125.97 (28.63)	3.83	126.18 (24.84)	4.02	0.05
(iii) Chemical Fertilizer	419.41 (98.33)	12.76	342.96 (108.41)	10.93	4.20*
(iv) Pesticides	87.77 (38.16)	2.67	77.04 (46.50)	2.46	1.41
(v) Seeds Cost	117.50 (22.50)	3.57	114.40 (21.76)	3.65	0.81
(vi) Farm Manure	183.36 (88.31)	5.58	140.38 (67.87)	4.48	3.30*
(vii) Cost of Irrigation	26.59 (3.39)	0.81	26.35 (4.25)	0.84	0.35
(viii) Interest on Working Capital	123.39 (15.76)	3.75	119.06 (14.61)	3.79	1.67
Cost A	2309.84	70.25	2197.46	70.06	–
Rent	824.62 (83.38)	25.08	778.64 (74.35)	24.82	3.43*
Interest on Fixed Capital excluding Land Revenue, Cesses and Taxes, Depreciation of Implements and machinery	153.40	4.67	160.62	5.12	
Cost C (Total)	3287.86 (500.79)	100.00	3136.72 (411.03)	100.00	
Yield per Acre in Kg	2367.35 (235.03)		2248.60 (237.98)		2.89*
Yield per Acre in Rs.	5795.35 (585.18)		5470.96 (435.93)		3.82*
Net Income per Acre in Rs.	2507.49 (702.50)		2334.24 (508.24)		1.72

Note: Figures in parentheses represent standard deviation.
* Indicates significance at 5 per cent level.

The table 4.3 shows that IR 20 variety yielded 2,367.35 kg of rice per acre, bringing in a revenue of Rs. 5,795.35. The net income over the total cost (Rs. 3,287.86) worked out to be Rs. 2,507.49 per acre. On the other hand, CO 37 variety had a physical turn-out of 2,248.60 kg, resulting in a monetary return of Rs. 5,470.96 per acre. The net income received against the total cost incurred (Rs. 3,136.72) was Rs. 2,334.24. The figures prove that the IR 20 variety performed significantly better than the CO 37 variety in terms of total yield (both physical and monetary) per acre. Besides, the total cost of cultivation was also higher by Rs. 151.14 per acre for the former variety, emphasising the need for a greater inputs use for its cultivation.

In both cases, operational cost formed about 70 per cent of the total cost. The pattern of average amount expended on variable inputs for the cultivation of the two varieties corresponded to each other. The use of chemical fertilizers and farm manures and rent differed significantly between the two varieties. Expenditure on human labour assumed a major share of the total cost in the case of IR 20 (37.28%) and CO 37 (39.89%) rice. Rent constituted nearly 25 per cent of the total cost in both cases. It was followed by expenses on chemical fertilizer, farm manure, interest on fixed capital, bullock labour and other variable inputs. The expenses on rent, chemical fertilizer and farm manures differed significantly between the two varieties. As argued by Junankar,[11] the difference in rent within the same area may be due to the imperfections in land market. The greater responsiveness of IR 20 variety to chemical fertilizer and farm manure explains the significant difference in the costs incurred on them by the two cultivators.[12] In brief, although its cost of cultivation was higher, IR 20 variety certainly did better than CO 37, both yield-wise and revenue-wise. The result of Kalirajan[13] contradicted this finding. He found CO 37 rice to be doing better than IR 20 rice in Coimbatore district. Variable cost accounted for about 70 per cent of the total cost in both cases. Human labour constituted the major cost component. Rajagopalan, et al.,[14] Harrison[15] and Subramaniyan[16] reported similar findings. It was followed by rent, chemical fertilizer, farm manure and other inputs.

Figure 4.1 picturises the operational cost structure of IR 20 and CO 37 varieties of rice.

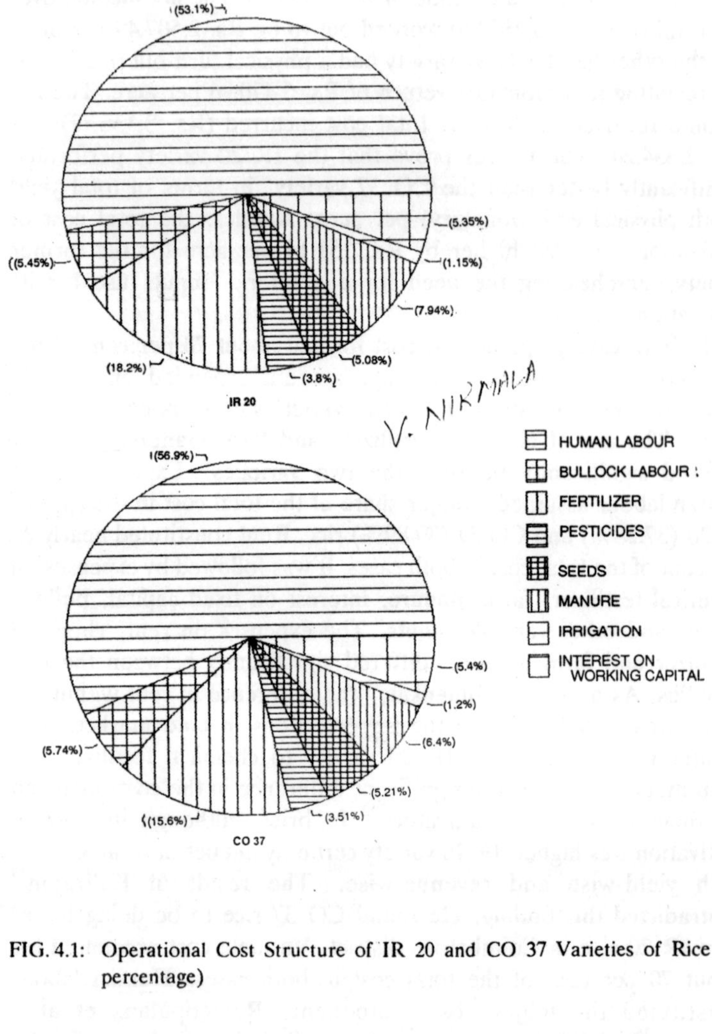

FIG. 4.1: Operational Cost Structure of IR 20 and CO 37 Varieties of Rice (in percentage)

Table 4.3.1 furnishes information on the average cost and return structure of large farmers and small farmers cultivating IR 20 variety of rice.

TABLE 4.3.1: Cost and Return Structure per Acre of IR 20 Farmer Groups, Rabi 1985-86

Cost Components	Small Farmers		Large Farmers		t-Value between Farmer Groups
	Value in Rs.	%	Value in Rs.	%	
(i) Human Labour (including Family Labour)	1271.77 (249.55)	37.64	1095.18 (160.66)	36.17	4.12*
(ii) Bullock Labour	132.84 (29.06)	3.93	106.40 (15.14)	3.51	5.88*
(iii) Chemical Fertilizer	427.27 (106.23	12.64	397.04 (66.29)	13.11	1.69
(iv) Pesticides	95.15 (31.75)	2.82	66.77 (46.23)	2.21	2.90*
(v) Seeds Cost	117.37 (20.71)	3.47	117.86 (26.94)	3.89	0.08
(vi) Farm Manure	179.52 (84.02)	5.31	194.26 (98.47)	6.42	0.68
(vii) Cost of Irrigation	26.64 (3.68)	0.79	26.44 (2.42)	0.87	0.31
(viii) Interest on Working Capital	124.81 (16.79)	3.69	119.32 (11.42)	3.94	1.85
Cost A	2375.37	70.29	2123.27	70.12	
Rent	833.81 (88.32)	24.68	798.43 (60.12)	26.37	2.26*
Interest on Fixed Capital excluding Land Revenue, Cesses and Taxes, Depreciation of Implements and Machinery	169.96	5.03	106.36	3.51	
Cost C (Total)	3379.14 (525.69)	100.00	3028.06 (294.63)	100.00	
Yield per Acre in kg	2422.01 (232.09)		2213.69 (164.46)		4.95*
Yield per Acre in Rs.	5757.28 (608.01)		5903.72 (499.03)		1.21
Net Income per Acre in Rs.	2378.14 (724.51)		2875.66 (465.99)		5.23*

Note: Figures in parentheses represent standard deviation.

* Indicates significance at 5 per cent level.

The per acre physical and monetary returns differed significantly between the large farms and small farms. Small farmers realised a physical output of 2,422.01 kg and a monetary return of Rs. 5,757.28 per acre. They earned a net return of Rs. 2,378.14. On the other hand, the quantity of rice harvested by large farmers was 2,213.69 kg per acre. However, the revenue earned (i.e., Rs. 5,903.72) by them was greater by Rs. 146.44 compared to the small farmers. The net income received by large farmers was Rs. 2,875.66, which was Rs. 497.52 more than the earnings of small farmers. The total cost incurred by the former was lower (Rs. 3,028.06) than the amount spent by the latter (Rs. 3,379.14). The resulting difference was Rs. 351.08 per acre. The analysis indicated that although small farmers incurred a higher cost of cultivation and obtained a larger quantity of output per acre, the large farmers had a definite advantage over them in terms of monetary gains. The study of Subramaniyan[17] supports this finding.

The expenditure on inputs exhibited almost a similar pattern in both cases. Variable cost formed about 70 per cent of their total cost. Human labour constituted the major cost component, accounting for more than 35 per cent of the total cost. Rajagopalan, et al.,[18] and Harrison[19] reported similar results. Rent was the next important item of expenditure, followed by chemical fertilizers, farm manure and other inputs. The expenditure on human labour, bullock labour, pesticides and rent differed significantly between the two farms. The expense on human labour per acre was higher on small farms, due to the more intensive use of family labour. The difference in bullock labour cost may be because of the ownership of bullock pair by the small farmers. The difference in pesticides cost arises out of the greater plant protection measures taken by the small farmers to ensure a good yield. Probably, the rent paid within the same area differed due to the existence of imperfect land market in the village.

An over-all glance at the table shows that although small farmers incurred a higher cost of production and yielded larger output, it was the large farmers who earned greater monetary benefits. The higher production per acre on small farms resulted from a more intensive use of inputs and better supervision of the farms. However, it was the large farmers who earned greater profits than the small farmers. This may be due to their better credit position, storage and other facilities, which enable them to wait for the maximum price for their produce. The expenses on input factors showed a similar tendency for the two classes of farmers. The difference between the two farmer groups in terms of human and bullock labour cost, pesticides cost, rent, physical yield and net income per acre emerged statistically significant at five per cent level.

Figure 4.2 illustrates the cost and return structure of IR 20 and CO 37 varieties of rice.

Note: TF — Total Farmers;
LF — Large Farmers; and
SF — Small Farmers.

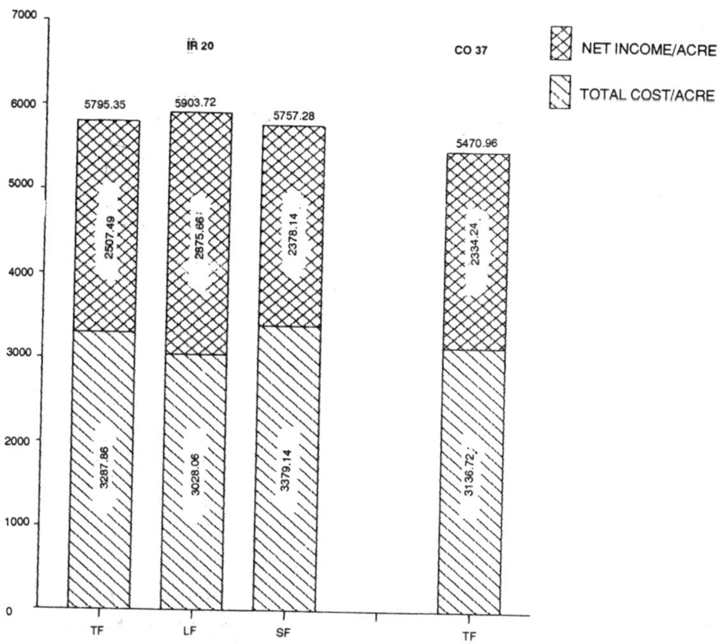

FIG. 4.2: Cost and Return Structure of IR 20 and CO 37 Varieties of Rice

4.4 Economics of Rice Cultivation

Table 4.4 contains details of the economics of cultivating IR 20 and CO 37 rice varieties in Gokilapuram.

TABLE 4.4: Economics of IR 20 and CO 37 Rice Cultivation per acre, Rabi 1985-86

Particulars	IR 20 Rice		CO 37 Rice	
	Unit in Qtls.	Value in Rs.	Unit in Qtls.	Value in Rs.
1. Output per Acre	23.68		22.49	
(i) Main product		5512.78		5206.52
(ii) By-product (Straw)		282.57		264.45
2. Gross Return		5795.35		5470.97
3. Total Operating Cost (Cost A)		2309.84		2197.46
4. Net Return over Cost A		3485.51		3273.48
5. Cost C		3287.86		3136.72
6. Net Return over Cost C		2507.49		2334.22
7. Cost of Production per Qtl. (Cost A)		97.54		97.71
8. Cost of Production per Qtl. (Cost C)		138.85		139.47
9. Input-Output Ratio (Cost A)		2.51		2.48
10. Input-Output Ratio (Cost C)		1.76		1.74
11. Cost-Benefit Ratio (Cost C)		0.76		0.74

The input-output ratio in terms of operational cost and total cost was found to be Rs. 2.51 and Rs. 1.76 for IR 20 and Rs. 2.48 and Rs. 1.74 per acre for CO 37, respectively. The cost-benefit ratio for IR 20 variety showed that each rupee expended resulted in a benefit of Re. 0.76 per acre. Likewise, the benefit was worth Re. 0.74 for CO 37 rice. This projects the superiority of the former variety in terms of the benefits received.

The economics of cultivating the two varieties of rice revealed that the cultivation of IR 20 variety would be more beneficial to rice farmers in terms of both yield and profit per acre. However, the total cost was also higher for the variety, indicating the requirement of a more intensive use of inputs for its cultivation.

Table 4.4.1 presents comparative information on the economics of raising IR 20 rice by the small and large farmer groups in Gokilapuram.

TABLE 4.4.1: Economics of IR 20 Rice Cultivation per acre by Farmer Groups, Rabi 1985-86

Particulars	Small Farmers		Large Farmers	
	Unit in Qtls.	Value in Rs.	Unit in Qtls.	Value in Rs.
1. Output per Acre	24.22		22.14	
(i) Main product		5484.37		5593.65
(ii) By-product (Straw)		272.92		310.07
2. Gross Return		5757.29		5903.72
3. Total Operating Cost (Cost A)		2375.37		2123.27
4. Net Return over Cost A		3381.92		3780.45
5. Cost C		3379.14		3028.06
6. Net Return over Cost C		2378.15		2875.66
7. Cost of Production per Qtl. (Cost A)		98.07		95.90
8. Cost of Production per Qtl. (Cost C)		139.52		136.77
9. Input-Output Ratio (Cost A)		2.42		2.78
10. Input-Output Ratio (Cost C)		1.70		1.95
11. Cost-Benefit Ratio (Cost C)		0.70		0.95

The input and output ratios and cost-benefit ratios projected a similar picture for the two IR 20 farmer groups. The input-output ratio per acre in terms of operational cost and total cost was Rs. 2.42 and Rs. 1.70 on small farms and Rs. 2.78 and Rs. 1.95 on large farms, respectively. Small farmers enjoyed a benefit of Re. 0.70 over a rupee spent on cultivation, while the profit gained by the large farmers was Re. 0.95.

Thus, it may be clearly seen that although the cost of production and output per acre on small farms were higher, it was the large farmers who enjoyed greater monetary benefits. This could be the outcome of the better economic and institutional position of large farmers compared to the small farmers, who generally experience these problems.

NOTES

1. R.N. Poduval, "Adoption of New Technology", *Foodgrains Economy of Tamil Nadu: Problems and Prospects*, Emerald Publishers, Madras, 1987, p. 32.
2. K. Kalirajan and R.T. Shand, "Location Specific Research: Rice Technology in India", *Land Economics*, Vol.58, No.4, November 1982, pp. 537-546.
3. G. Subramaniyan, *Cotton in Madurai District: An Econometric Analysis*, Northern Book Centre, New Delhi, 1987.
4. James Quigley Harrison, Agricultural Modernization and Income Distribution: An Economic Analysis of the Impact of New Seed Varieties on the Crop Production of Large and Small Farms in India, (mimeo), Ph. D., Princeton University, 1972.
5. J.P. Singh and K.V. Govindaraju, "New Technology of Paddy Yield: Adoption and Yield Differentials", *New Seeds: Adoption and Yield*, Sterling Publishers Pvt. Ltd., New Delhi, 1979, pp. 3-89.
6. L.J. Unnevehr and M.L. Stanford, *Technology and the Demand for Women's Labour in Asian Rice Farming*, Paper presented at the Conference on Women in Rice Farming Systems, International Rice Research Institute, September 26-30, 1983, p. 2.
7. Subramaniyan, loc. cit.
8. P.K. Aiyasamy, V. Rajagopalan and R. Sundaresan, "Economic Appraisal of Pattern of Labour Utilisation in Different Tracts of Tamil Nadu", *Southern Economic Review*, Vol.5, No.1, July 1975, pp. 31-49.
9. Unnevehr and Stanford, op. cit., p. 2.
10. Subramaniyan, op. cit.
11. P.N. Junankar, "Do Indian Farmers Maximise Profits?", *Journal of Development Studies*, Vol.17, No.1, October 1980, pp. 48-61.
12. Poduval, loc. cit.
13. K. Kalirajan, "The Contribution of Location Specific Research to Agricultural Productivity", *Indian Journal of Agricultural Economics*, Vol. 35, No.4, October-December 1980, pp. 8-16.
14. V. Rajagopalan, et al., *Studies on Cost of Production of Major Crops in Tamil Nadu*, Department of Agricultural Economics, Tamil Nadu Agricultural University, Coimbatore, 1978.
15. Harrison, loc. cit.
16. Subramaniyan, loc. cit.
17. Subramaniyan, Ibid.
18. Rajagopalan, et al., loc. cit.
19. Harrison, loc. cit.

5

DETERMINANTS OF YIELD, YIELD GAP AND YIELD CONSTRAINTS

This chapter attempts to identify the major determinants of yield of IR 20 and CO 37 varieties of rice and of small and large categories of IR 20 farmers in the rabi season, 1985-86, of Gokilapuram. It also examines the yield gap arising out of the difference between maximum and the average yield at farm level under each variety. It further investigates the yield constraints which prevent the IR 20 and CO 37 rice growers from achieving the potential yield at farm level in the village.

5.1 Determinants of Yield

A Cobb-Douglas type[1] of yield function was used to estimate the main factors determining the yields of the two rice varieties and at the large and small IR 20 farms. The yield function was fitted with yield as the dependent variable and input variables along with other socio-economic factors as the independent variables. The identification and measurement of qualitative factors being difficult, dummy variables were introduced to represent them in the model. The regression models were first run separately for the total sample of each variety and then for each of the two IR 20 farmer groups.

To identify the major factors associated with the variations in rice yield, different forms of regression models (with and without logarithm) were estimated, using different combinations of explanatory variables. The factors having signs contradictory to theoretical expectations and emerging statistically insignificant were eliminated. Finally, only the following five variables were left to explain the variations in yield: (i) total labour, (ii) fertilizer, (iii) pesticides, (iv) capital flows, and (v) net return. Net return of the previous year was included as one of the explanatory variables, as it represents economic incentive to the farmers to increase rice yield.[2]

The regression model fitted to study the determinants of rice yield was of the form:

$$\log Y = \beta_0 + \beta_1 \log X_1 + \beta_2 \log X_2 + \beta_3 \log X_3 + \beta_4 \log X_4 + \beta_5 \log X_5 + U$$

where,

Y = yield per acre in kg.,
X_1 = total labour per acre in mandays,
X_2 = fertilizer per acre in kg.,
X_3 = pesticides per acre in kg.,
X_4 = capital flows per acre in Rs.,
X_5 = net return per acre in Rs. of the previous harvest year, and
U = disturbance term with $N(0, \sigma^2)$.

The above equation was estimated based on the principle of least squares.

Further, Chow test[3] was adopted to examine whether structural difference existed between IR 20 and CO 37 varieties of rice and between the large farmers and small farmers cultivating the IR 20 rice. The formula used was:

$$F^* = \frac{\Sigma e^2 - (\Sigma e_1^2 + \Sigma e_2^2)/K}{(\Sigma e_1^2 + \Sigma e_2^2)/n_1 + n_2 - 2K}$$

where,

K = number of parameters including the intercept term,
Σe^2 = unexplained sum of squares for pooled relations,
Σe_1^2 = unexplained sum of squares for small farmers/IR 20 variety,
Σe_2^2 = unexplained sum of squares for large farmers/CO 37 variety, and
$n_1 + n_2$ = total number of observations.

Table 5.1 presents the estimates of regression analysis for small farmers, large farmers and total farmers cultivating IR 20 rice.

In the case of total farmers, the independent variable explained about 55 per cent of the observed variability in rice yield. All the five variables had a positive impact on yield. Inputs fertilizers, pesticides, capital flows and net return were significantly related to the dependent variable. Net return was the most influential factor, indicating that profits of the previous harvest year contributed the major incentive to farmers to increase rice yield. One per cent increase in the factor resulted in 0.1694 per cent increase in yield. The other important determinants of yield were capital flows (0.087%) and fertilizer (0.064%). The over-all regression model emerged statistically significant at five per cent level.

TABLE 5.1: Regression Coefficients for IR 20 Variety of Rice

Variables	Parameter Estimates		
	Small Farmers	Large Farmers	Total Farmers
Intercept	2.1988	2.0178	2.3899
$\log X_1$	0.0652	0.0330	0.0289
	(1.2719)	(0.7882)	(0.6717)
$\log X_2$	0.1098*	0.0589	0.0639*
	(2.8288)	(1.6266)	(1.9134)
$\log X_3$	0.0039	0.0038	0.0191*
	(0.3511)	(0.6430)	(2.6655)
$\log X_4$	0.0615*	0.0585*	0.0872*
	(2.7859)	(3.1759)	(4.7509)
$\log X_5$	0.1958*	0.2915*	0.1694*
	(7.2539)	(6.9051)	(7.0066)
R^2	0.5339	0.8118	0.5458
F-Value	17.7329	22.5662	24.7891
Residual Sum of Squares	0.0552	0.0038	0.0779
No. of Observations	74	26	100

The analysis revealed that 81 per cent of the variations in yield in the case of large farmers were jointly caused by the five explanatory variables. Net return and capital flows were statistically significant at five per cent level, indicating that one per cent increase in these factors could increase yield per acre by 0.2915 per cent and 0.0585 per cent respectively. Fertilizer, total labour and pesticides also had a positive but insignificant impact on yield. The *F*-value showed that the model was statistically significant at five per cent level.

As far as the small farmers are concerned, the explanatory variables exercised positive influence on the dependent variable. The coefficients of net return (0.1958), fertilizer (0.1098) and capital flows (0.0615) were significant at five per cent level. The five variables together accounted for nearly 53 per cent of the variations in yield.

The regression model was statistically significant at five per cent level.

In general, the independent variables together explained more than 50 per cent of the observed variability in rice yield of the two farmer groups and total farmers growing IR 20 variety. The five independent factors had positive impact on yield. Net return was the most significant factor influencing the yield of rice in all three cases. It emphasized the role of economic incentive as an important stimuli to the farmers to increase rice yield. This result is similar to the findings of Kuo, Wu and Li[4] and Subramaniyan.[5] Capital flows and fertilizer were the next important determinants of yield. It is to be noted that the coefficients corresponding to labour emerged positive as expected, but insignificant, in all three cases. This may be due to excess application of labour input by the farmers. Further, it could be attributed to high degree of correlation (multicollinearity) between labour and capital flows in all three cases, which was 0.51 for large farmers, 0.61 for small farmers and 0.64 for total farmers. To overcome the difficulty of multicollinearity, it was not possible to drop out either labour or capital flows from the regression model, as it would have led to mis-specification of the model. All the three regression models were statistically significant.

Using Chow test, an attempt was made to identify whether structural difference existed between small farmers and large farmers producing the IR 20 rice. The results are given in Table 5.2.

TABLE 5.2: Structural Difference between IR 20 Large Farmers and Small Farmers

Σe^2	Σe_1^2	Σe_2^2	n_1+n_2-2K	F^*	$F(6, 88)$ at 5% level	Inference
0.0779	0.0552	0.0037	88	0.4714	2.18	No structural difference exists between small and large farmer groups growing IR 20 rice.

The result of the Chow test shows that the computed F-value (0.47) worked out to be less than the table F-value (2.18) at five per cent level for (6.88) degrees of freedom. This implied that there was no indication of structural difference between the small farmers and large farmers cultivating IR 20 variety of rice.

Table 5.3 provides the estimates of the regression analysis for total farmers growing CO 37 variety of rice.

TABLE 5.3: Regression Coefficients for CO 37 Variety of Rice

Variables	Parameter Estimates
	Total Farmers
Intercept	1.8414
$\log X_1$	0.5987*
	(6.2412)
$\log X_2$	0.0196
	(1.1436)
$\log X_3$	0.0439
	(0.9111)
$\log X_4$	0.0283*
	(2.0359)
$\log X_5$	0.0335
	(1.3039)
$\bar{R}^2$	0.8953
F-Value	84.8464
Residual Sum of Squares	0.0074
No. of Observations	50

Note: Figures in parentheses represent *t*-value.
* Indicates significance at 5 per cent level.

The analysis revealed that the included explanatory variables together caused about 90 per cent of the variations in the yield of CO 37 rice. The model emerged statistically significant at five per cent level. The independent variables had positive effect on yield. Total labour was observed to be the most influential factor, implying that one per cent increase in the variable could increase yield by 0.5987 per cent. It was followed by pesticides (0.0439) and net return (0.0335). Labour and capital flows were significantly related to rice yield.

In sum, all the independent variables had a positive influence on the yield of CO 37 rice. The regression model was highly significant. Yield was highly responsive and significantly related to total labour. Unlike under IR 20 rice where net return and capital flows were the important yield determinants, total labour followed by pesticides and net return had greater effect on CO 37 rice yield.

To examine if structural difference existed between IR 20 and CO 37 varieties of rice, Chow test was adopted. The results of the test are reported in Table 5.4.

TABLE 5.4: Structural Difference between IR 20 and CO 37 Varieties of Rice

Σe^2	Σe_1^2	Σe_2^2	n_1+n_2-2K	F^*	$F(6, 138)$ at 5% level	Inference
0.1151	0.0779	0.0076	138	7.9860	2.10	Sructural difference exists between IR 20 and CO 37 varieties of rice

The calculated F-value worked out to be about 7.99, while the table F-value was 2.10. As the computed value was higher than the table value, it indicated that structural difference existed between IR 20 and CO 37 varieties of rice.

A Cobb-Douglas type of yield function was used as the analytical tool to identify the factors causing structural differences between the yields of the two rice varieties. The sample farmers had reported the incidence of pest-attack on both varieties of rice during the survey. Since most of the sample participants had applied pesticides almost as recommended by the extension officials, representation of the factor plant protection in the Cobb-Douglas function either in physical terms or in monetary terms, could not explain yield differences significantly. Therefore, dummy variable D_2 was included to take care of this factor. It enters the yield function as a shift variable, showing that absolute difference between pest-attacked and pest-free yield is independent of the quantity of inputs included in the equation. Dummy variable D_1 was introduced to represent varietal difference. The coefficients of dummy variables, along with constant term, provide an estimate of the shifts in the yield. The yield function used for the analysis was of the form:

$$\log Y = \alpha_0 + \alpha_1 D_1 + \alpha_2 D_2 + \alpha_3 D_{12} + \sum_{i=1}^{5} \log X_i(\beta_i + D_1\gamma_i) + U$$

where,

Y = yield per acre in kg.,
X_1 = total labour input per acre in mandays,
X_2 = fertilizer used per acre in kg.,
X_3 = pesticides applied per acre in kg.,

X_4 = capital flows per acre in Rs., which is the sum of depreciation, maintenance and opportunity cost of capital stock,
X_5 = net return per acre in Rs. of the previous harvest year,
D_1 = varietal dummy taking value one for CO 37 and zero for IR 20 variety of rice,
D_2 = pest-attack dummy taking value one for pest-attack and zero otherwise,
D_{12} = interaction between the dummy variable D_1 and D_2, and
U = disturbance term with $N(0, \sigma^2)$.

The yield function was estimated by using the method of least squares. Table 5.5 gives the results of the regression analysis.

TABLE 5.5: Tests of the Stability of Intercept and Slope between IR 20 and CO 37 Varieties of Rice

Variables	Parameter Estimates
α_0 Intercept	2.1811
D_1 (Variety Dummy)	−0.0388* (−6.0559)
D_2 (Pest-Attack Dummy)	−0.0044 (−0.9879)
D_{12} (Interaction Dummy)	0.0118 (0.9726)
$\log X_1$	0.0584 (1.7979)
$\log X_2$	0.1071* (4.0661)
$\log X_3$	0.0029 (0.4699)
$\log X_4$	0.0629* (4.2818)
$\log X_5$	0.2072* (11.2186)
$D_1 \log X_1$	0.3911* (3.4257)
$D_1 \log X_2$	−0.0921* (−2.3291)
$D_1 \log X_3$	0.1525* (1.9861)
$D_1 \log X_4$	−0.0378 (−1.3489)
$D_1 \log X_5$	−0.1971* (−4.2076)
R^2	0.7292
F-Value	31.8637
Residual Sum of Squares	0.0688
No. of Observations	150

Note: Figures in parentheses represent t-value.
* Indicates significance at 5 per cent level.

The analysis showed that the slope coefficients relating to inputs and the coefficients corresponding to intercept dummy (i.e., varietal dummy) were statistically significant between the two varieties. This indicated that: (i) the yield curve of IR 20 variety had shifted neutrally in relation to that of CO 37 variety, and (ii) the conventional factors of production were responsible for the difference in yield between the two varieties. The coefficients corresponding to pest-attack dummy and interaction dummy emerged statistically insignificant. This implied that pest-attack was not responsible for the difference in yield between the two varieties. This may be due to the effective plant protection measures adopted by the sample farmers.

In the case of IR 20 rice, all explanatory variables had positive impact on yield per acre. Net return was the most influential variable in relation to yield. A percentage increase in the factor was capable of increasing yield by 0.2072 per cent. An increase in fertilizer by one per cent could increase yield by 0.1071 per cent. It was followed by capital flows, an additional percentage of which could increase yield by 0.0629 per cent. These three variables were statistically significant at five per cent level.

The result relating to CO 37 variety showed that structural difference between the two varieties was caused by the variables total labour, fertilizer, pesticides and net return. This indicated that if total labour was increased by one per cent, yield per acre of IR 20 variety could be increased by 0.06 per cent and that of CO 37 by 0.45 per cent. An additional percentage of fertilizer was capable of increasing the yield of IR 20 rice by 0.11 per cent and of CO 37 by only 0.02 per cent. This could be because the IR 20 variety is highly responsive to fertilizer compared to CO 37.[6] If the use of pesticides was increased by one per cent, yield of IR 20 rice could be increased by 0.003 per cent and of CO 37 by 0.16 per cent. In other words, while a percentage increase in pesticides and total labour had a relatively greater effect on the yield of CO 37 variety, a similar increase in fertilizer and net return had a more favourable impact on the yield of IR 20 rice. The F-value indicated that the regression model was highly significant.

In brief, structural difference between IR 20 and CO 37 varieties of rice existed both at the intercept and slope levels. As the coefficient of dummy variable corresponding to the variety of rice was statistically significant, it could be inferred that variety was responsible for the difference in yield of the two rice varieties. The insignificant coefficient of the dummy variable corresponding to pest-attack indicated that it was not responsible for the difference in yield between the two varieties. At the slope level, differences in yields were caused by the difference in levels of input application by the growers of the two rice varieties. The inputs causing the differences were total labour, fertilizer, pesticides and net return. Kalirajan and Shand[7] arrived at a different conclusion in their study. They found the incidence of BPH (Brown Plant Hopper) pest rather than the differences in variety or input use to be the crucial factor causing the difference in the yields of exotic (IR 20) and location-specific varieties (ADT 31 and CO 37) of rice in Coimbatore district. This could be due to the difference in study area and the period of study selected.

5.2 Yield Gap and Yield Constraints

This section of the chapter deals with the yield gap analysis with respect to IR 20 and CO 37 varieties of rice and the identification of the main factors that act as constraints to the achievement of potential (maximum) yield at farm level in Gokilapuram. In the study, Yield gap II has been studied. It was identified as the difference between maximum yield and average yield obtained under farmers' conditions in the village.

Figure 5.1 diagrammatically projects the observed yield gap at farm level between the potential yield and actual yield in the village, with respect to IR 20 and CO 37 rice cultivation.

In the case of IR 20 rice cultivation in Gokilapuram, the maximum yield reaped was 27.11 quintals while the average yield was 23.57 quintals per acre. This resulted in a yield gap of 3.54 quintals per acre. On the other hand, the maximum yield obtained by the best CO 37 farmer was 25.20 quintals, while the actual yield was 22.39 quintals. This caused a yield gap of 2.81 quintals per acre.

Thus, the yield gap analysis revealed that there was a difference between the maximum yield and actual yield under both varieties of rice in the village. Besides, the yield gap identified under IR 20 was larger compared to CO 37 variety.

Today, majority of the Indian farmers are aware of the new technology. Whatever the variety cultivated (i.e., IR 20 or CO 37), their foremost aim is to reap maximum yield. However, not all farmers are able to attain the potential yield at farms. The reason may be the several bio-physical and socio-economic bottle-necks which limit yield increases at farm level. By and large, the important yield constraints under farmers' conditions may be – (a) bio-physical, and (b) socio-economic. Bio-physical constraints include — (i) water shortage, (ii) soil fertility, (iii) problems of the soil, (iv) insects, (v) weeds, (vi) variety, and (vii) cultural practices. Socio-economic constraints comprise the following factors — (i) credit, (ii) non-availability of inputs (seed), (iii) economic bahaviour, (iv) risk aversion, (v) knowledge, (vi) institutions, and (vii) traditional methods.

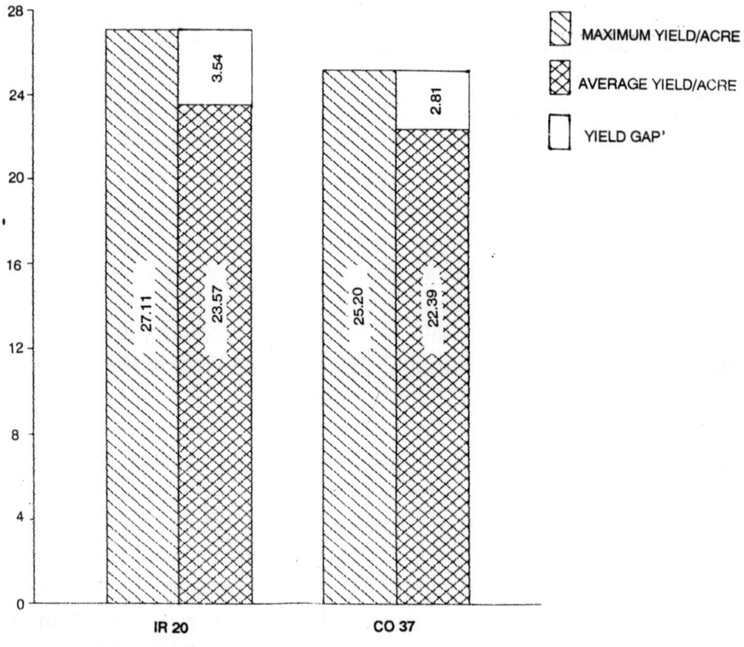

FIG 5.1: Yield Gap of IR 20 and CO 37 Varieties of Rice

Garrett's ranking technique[8] was adopted to identify the main constraints to potential yield in the village. The sample farmers were requested to rank the constraints encountered by them as per priority. The order of merit assigned to each constraint by the respondents were converted into ranks by using the formula:

$$\text{Per Cent Position} = \frac{100\,(R_{ij} - 0.5)}{N_j}$$

where,

R_{ij} = rank given by the jth individual for the ith factor, and
N_j = number of factors ranked by the jth individual.

The per cent position of each rank thus obtained was converted into scores, by referring to the Garrett's ranking table. The scores of all respondents for each factor was then added together and divided by the number of respondents experiencing that particular constraint. The mean scores of each factor thus arrived at, were arranged in a descending order and the corresponding ranks allotted.

Of the various bio-physical and socio-economic constraints listed, the respondents growing IR 20 and CO 37 varieties of rice in Gokilapuram, reported six factors to be the major yield constraints restricting them from achieving the potential yield in the study area. It included three bio-physical factors, viz., (i) water shortage, (ii) insects, and (iii) weeds, and three socio-economic factors, viz., (i) credit, (ii) non-availability of inputs (seeds), and (iii) traditional methods.

Table 5.6 highlights the yield constraints reported by the IR 20 rice farmers.

In the case of IR 20 variety, 53 per cent of the sample farmers stated insects to be the main constraint to the potential yield at farm level. Owing to the scantiness of rains during the rabi season, 1985-86, in the village, water shortage was reported to be the second major constraint by 69 per cent of them. About 27 per cent of the farmers pointed out non-availability of inputs (mainly certified seeds) in time to be the third constraint. It was followed by the constraints non-availability of credit when required (35%), weeds (21%) and traditional methods (9%), respectively.

Table 5.7 presents the main yield constraints to the potential yield of CO 37 variety of rice in Gokilapuram.

TABLE 5.6: Yield Constraints of IR 20 Rice Farmers in Gokilapuram, Rabi 1985-86

Yield Constraints	Total Score	Mean Score	Rank	No. of Farmers Responded
1. Insects	3029	57.15	1	53 (53.00)
2. Water Shortage	3660	53.04	2	69 (69.00)
3. Non-Availability of Inputs (Seeds)	1353	50.11	3	27 (27.00)
4. Credit	1469	41.97	4	35 (35.00)
5. Weeds	861	41.00	5	21 (21.00)
6. Traditional Methods	322	35.78	6	9 (9.00)

Note: Figures in parentheses represent percentage to total sample farmers.

TABLE 5.7: Yield Constraints of CO 37 Rice Farmers in Gokilapuram, Rabi 1985-86

Yield Constraints	Total Score	Mean Score	Rank	No. of Farmers Responded
1. Water Shortage	2396	63.05	1	38 (76.00)
2. Insects	1112	50.55	2	22 (44.00)
3. Credit	985	46.90	3	21 (42.00)
4. Traditional Methods	770	42.78	4	18 (36.00)
5. Weeds	681	40.06	5	17 (34.00)
6. Non-Availability of Inputs (Seeds)	556	39.71	6	14 (28.00)

Note: Figures in parentheses represent percentage to total sample farmers.

With regard to CO 37, water shortage was cited to be the major constraint to potential yield by 76 per cent of the sample farmers.

This was attributed to the deficit rainfall during the study period. Problem of insects was quoted to be the second factor affecting the achievement of maximum yield by 44 per cent of the farmers. Non-availability of credit when necessary (42%) and traditional methods (36%) were assigned the subsequent positions as yield constraints. They were followed by the other constraints, namely, weeds (34%) and non-availability of inputs, i.e. certified seeds, (28%) when required.

Thus, it may be observed that majority of the farmers producing the two varieties of rice reported the bio-physical factors insects and water shortage to be the major yield constraints in the village during rabi 1985-86. This was followed by the other factors, with minor variations in the priority assigned by the producers of the two varieties. This suggests that yield gap between the potential yield and average yield under farmers' conditions in the village can be reduced by overcoming the constraints reported by them. This would help all farmers to enjoy the potential benefits from the cultivation of IR 20 and CO 37 rice varieties. For this, the existing programmes specific to the problems should be implemented more strictly.

NOTES

1. A Cobb-Douglas type of regression model was used due to the simplicity and ease with which elasticities can be estimated. For details on the Cobb-Douglas functional form, refer J.R. Anderson and N.S. Jodha, "On Cobb-Douglas and Related Myths", *Economic and Political Weekly,* Review of Agriculture, Vol. VIII, June 1973, pp. A-65-A-75.
2. The variable 'net return' is subject to recall bias. For a brief discussion on the inclusion of the factor as an explanatory variable in the regression model, see Yi-Chung Kuo, Carson Wu and Cheng Chang Li, "Rice Production in Taiwan's Agriculture", *Constraints to High Yields on Asian Rice Farms: An Interim Report,* International Rice Research Institute, Philippines, October 1977, pp. 177-201, and G. Subramaniyan, *Cotton in Madurai District: An Econometric Analysis,* Northern Book Centre, New Delhi, 1987, p. 101.
3. Gregory C. Chow, "Tests of Equality between Sets of Coefficients in Two Linear Regressions", *Econometrica,* Vol.28, No. 3, July 1960, pp. 591-605.
4. Kuo, Wu, Li, loc. cit.
5. Subramaniyan, op. cit.
6. R.N. Poduval, "Adoption of New Technology", *Foodgrain Economy of Tamil Nadu: Problems and Prospects,* Emerald Publishers, Madras, 1987, p. 32.
7. K. Kalirajan and R.T. Shand, "Location Specific Research: Rice Technology in India", *Land Economics,* Vol. 58, No. 4, November 1982, pp. 537-546.
8. Henry E. Garrett and R.S. Woodworth, "The Scaling of Mental Tests and Other Psychological Data", *Statistics in Psychology and Education,* Vakils, Feffer and Simons Ltd., Bombay, 1981, pp. 309-336.

6

FARM SIZE AND INCOME DISTRIBUTION

Since the publication of the Farm Management Survey reports in the mid-'50s, the issue focussed in discussion is the alleged relationship between farm size and productivity. The argument started with the publication of Sen's[1] paper in which he had stated that "by and large, productivity per acre decreases with the size of holding". Most of the studies in India in this regard, are based on aggregated as well as disaggregated Farm Management Survey data. Chattopadhyay and Rudra[2] expressed reservations about the universal validity of inverse relationship. Saini[3] confirmed the inverse relationship between farm size and productivity on the basis of disaggregated Farm Management data. A survey of related literature shows that studies at micro level are very scarce. Keeping this point in view, an attempt is made in this chapter to examine the relationship between farm size and productivity with reference to the cultivation of IR 20 and CO 37 varieties of rice in Gokilapuram during rabi 1985-86. It also examines the inequalities in distribution of net farm income from the cultivation of the two rice varieties.

6.1 Farm Size and Productivity

Regressions of various forms (simple linear, semi-log and double-log) were estimated to examine the relationship between the independent variable farm size (in terms of acreage) and dependent variable farm efficiency (in terms of output per acre, output per manday, average variable cost and average total cost). Among the farm efficiency variables, output per acre and output per manday represent productivity factors which the farmers seek to maximise, while average variable cost and average cost represent the cost factors which they try to minimise. The regressions were estimated on the basis of the principle of ordinary least squares. The results of all three forms of regression analysis are given in the chapter.

However, only the results of double-log regression analysis are discussed here. The results of simple and semi-log regression analysis were not considered for discussion due to the following reasons:

(a) low values of $\bar{R}^2$ and *F*-value; and
(b) identical signs of the regression coefficients in all the three forms.

Tables 6.1, 6.2 and 6.3 present the respective results of the simple, semi-log and double-log regression analysis for IR 20 rice.

TABLE 6.1: Estimated Regression Equation of the Form: $Y = \beta_0 + \beta_1 X$, IR 20 Rice Variety

Dependent Variable	Independent Variable	Regression Coefficient	$\bar{R}^2$	*F*-Value
1. Output per Acre	Acreage	−14.9391 (−3.1669)*	0.08	10.0288*
2. Output per Manday	Acreage	0.1013 (1.0620)	0.001	1.1270
3. Average Variable Cost	Acreage	−25.496 (−3.7290)*	0.12	13.9061*
4. Average Total Cost	Acreage	−35.2258 (3.5444)*	0.10	12.5629*

Note: Figures in parentheses represent *t*-value.
* Indicates significance at 5 per cent level.

TABLE 6.2: Estimated Regression Equation of the Form: $\log Y = \beta_0 + \beta_1 X$, IR 20 Rice Variety

Dependent Variable	Independent Variable	Regression Coefficient	$\bar{R}^2$	*F*-Value
1. Output per Acre	Acreage	-0.0063 (-3.2209)*	0.09	10.3747*
2. Output per Manday	Acreage	0.0056 (1.2102)	0.005	1.4646
3. Average Variable Cost	Acreage	-0.0109 (-3.8291)*	0.12	15.1482*
4. Average Total Cost	Acreage	-0.0105 (3.6643)*	0.11	13.4267*

Note: Figures in parentheses represent *t*-value.
* Indicates significance at 5 per cent level.

TABLE 6.3: Estimated Regression Equation of the Form: $\log Y = \beta_0 + \beta_1 \log X$, IR 20 Rice Variety

Dependent Variable	Independent Variable	Regression Coefficient	$\bar{R}^2$	*F*-Value
1. Output per Acre	Acreage	-0.0373 (-3.9254)*	0.13	15.4087*
2. Output per Manday	Acreage	0.0446 (1.9751)	0.03	3.9009
3. Average Variable Cost	Acreage	-0.0779 (-0.1688)*	0.27	38.0548*
4. Average Total Cost	Acreage	-0.0752 (-5.7488)*	0.24	33.0493*

Note: Figures in parentheses represent *t*-value.
* Indicates significance at 5 per cent level.

The relationship between farm size and output per acre was observed to be negative and significant. This implied that increase in acreage had a decreasing effect on land productivity. This finding is contradictory to the results of Hanumantha Rao[4] and Ghosh[5] for the post-Green Revolution period. A positive relationship was identified between farm size and output per manday. However, this relation was found to be statistically insignificant. Acreage and average variable cost and acreage and average total cost were inversely and significantly related. This indicated a decline in the cost factor in response to an expansion in farm size, owing to the emergence of economies of scale. The value of $\bar{R}^2$ ranged between about three per cent to 27 per cent in the four regression analysis. The regression models fitted for acreage and output per acre, acreage and average variable cost and acreage and average total cost emerged statistically significant at five per cent level.

Tables 6.4, 6.5 and 6.6 give the results of the different forms of regression analysis for CO 37 variety of rice.

The analysis revealed a significant and inverse relationship between farm size and output per acre. This indicated that productivity declined with an increase in acreage in the village. This result is contradictory to the findings of Hanumantha Rao[6] and Ghosh[7] who reported the prevalence of direct relations in the post-Green Revolution period, due to the adoption of new agricultural technology by farmers. Output per manday was negatively associated with farm size, implying a decline in labour productivity in response to an increase in acreage. However, the regression coefficient was quite low and statistically insignificant. Average variable cost and farm size and average total cost and farm size were negatively and significantly related. This indicated that an increase in farm size was accompanied by a decrease in the unit cost in rice farming. This may be explained by the setting-in of economies of scale. Less than 29 per cent of the observed variability in the dependent variables was caused by the independent variable in the four regressions. All regression models, except that of farm size and output per manday, emerged statistically significant at five per cent level.

TABLE 6.4: Estimated Regression Equation of the Form: log $Y = \beta_0 + \beta_1 X$, CO 37 Rice Variety

Dependent Variable	Independent Variable	Regression Coefficient	$\bar{R}^2$	*F*-Value
1. Output per Acre	Acreage	-38.2996 (-1.9761)	0.06	3.0950
2. Output per Manday	Acreage	-0.0870 (-1.3251)	0.02	1.7559
3. Average Variable Cost	Acreage	-72.4102 (-3.2907)*	0.17	10.8291*
4. Average Total Cost	Acreage	-100.9185 (-3.2421)*	0.16	10.5112*

Note: Figures in parentheses represent *t*-value.
* Indicates significance at 5 per cent level.

TABLE 6.5: Estimated Regression Equation of the Form: log $Y = \beta_0 + \beta_1 X$, CO 37 Rice Variety

Dependent Variable	Independent Variable	Regression Coefficient	$\bar{R}^2$	*F*-Value
1. Output per Acre	Acreage	-0.0156 (-2.0656)*	0.06	4.2670*
2. Output per Manday	Acreage	-0.0047 (-1.3242)	0.02	1.7535
3. Average Variable Cost	Acreage	-0.0323 (-3.2641)*	0.16	10.6542*
4. Average Total Cost	Acreage	-0.0316 (-3.2209)*	0.16	10.3746*

Note: Figures in parentheses represent *t*-value.
* Indicates significance at 5 per cent level.

TABLE 6.6: Estimated Regression Equation of the Form: $\log Y = \beta_0 + \beta_1 \log X$, CO 37 Rice Variety

Dependent Variable	Independent Variable	Regression Coefficient	$\bar{R}^2$	*F*-Value
1. Output per Acre	Acreage	-0.0446 (-2.4588)*	0.09	6.0459*
2. Output per Manday	Acreage	-0.0136 (-1.5616)	0.03	2.4387
3. Average Variable Cost	Acreage	-0.1002 (-4.4272)*	0.28	19.6009*
4. Average Total Cost	Acreage	-0.0976 (-4.3283)*	0.27	18.7342*

Note: Figures in parentheses represent *t*-value.
* Indicates significance at 5 per cent level.

The relationship between farm size and output per acre and farm size and average cost for both IR 20 and CO 37 varieties of rice are illustrated in Fig. 6.1. The relationship between acreage and output per manday is not represented diagrammatically due to the insignificant result.

To sum up, increase in farm size was followed by a significant decrease in land productivity with respect to IR 20 and CO 37 rice cultivation in Gokilapuram. This could be because as the area under cultivation expands, factors like entrepreneurship and input use get stretched over a larger area, resulting in their reduced efficiency. The relationship between acreage and labour productivity emerged negative in CO 37 and positive in IR 20 rice farming. However, the relationship was statistically insignificant under both the varieties. The cost variables declined significantly in relation to an increase in acreage in the case of the two varieties. This suggested a minimisation in the cost of cultivation arising out of economies of scale. Under both varieties, the independent variable explained less than 30 per cent of the variations in the farm efficiency variables. All regression models (except, output per manday and acreage) were statistically significant at five per cent level.

6.2 Distribution of Income

"Distribution of income being the end result of the working of the economic process, reflects all its aspects: level and pattern of

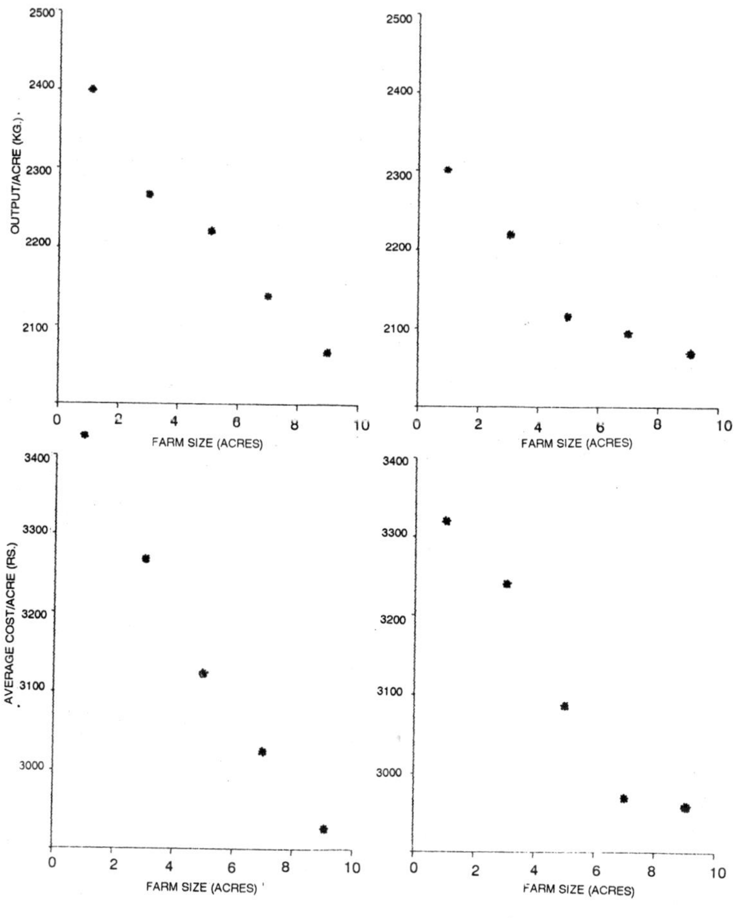

FIG. 6.1: Farm Size and Productivity

resource use, resource allocation and resource creation, real and monetary".[8] In this study, inequality of income distribution refers to the disparity in income earned from rice cultivation alone. This section investigates the distribution pattern of net income per acre among the cultivators of IR 20 and CO 37 varieties of rice in Gokilapuram, during rabi season, 1985-86. In this context, the hypothesis of inequality in the distribution of net income per acre from IR 20 and CO 37 rice cultivation was examined.

To examine the inequality in the distribution of net income among farmers growing IR 20 and CO 37 varieties of rice, Gini coefficient was used. It was worked out by using the formula:[9]

$$1+\frac{1}{n}-\frac{2}{n^2\bar{y}}(ny_1+(n-1)y_2+\cdots\cdots+2y_{n-1}+y_n)$$

where,

n = number of individuals,

y_i = income of individual rank $i(y_1 \leq y_2 \leq y_3 \ldots\ldots y_{n-1} \leq y_n)$, and

$\bar{y}$ = mean income.

Table 6.7 depicts the pattern of distribution of net income per acre among the sample farmers growing IR 20 and CO 37 varieties of rice in rabi season, 1985-86, and their respective Gini coefficients. In the study, net income refers to total income less total variable cost. The figures presented in the table were worked out by arranging the total sample farmers for each variety separately in ascending order according to their net incomes and then classifying them into decile groups. Next, the share of the total net income for each decile group was calculated and the cumulative percentages computed.

The Table 6.7 reveals that the net income per acre from IR 20 cultivation was generally high compared to CO 37 variety. In the bottom income groups, 30 per cent (decile group I-III) of the farmers received 20.11 per cent of the total net income from IR 20 cultivation. Of the total cultivators, 60 per cent of them (decile group I-VI) shared 49.01 per cent of the total net income, while the remaining 50.99 per cent was enjoyed by 40 per cent (decile group VII-X) of the top income group. The 20 per cent of large income earners (decile group IX-X) received more than quarter (27.81%) of the total net income. Thus, a major portion of the net income was shared by 40 per cent of the top income group of farmers than the remaining farmers (60%) who received only about half the total net income.

TABLE 6.7: Distribution of Net Income per Acre by Decile Groups of Sample Farmers and Gini Coefficients, Rabi 1985-86.

	IR 20		CO 37	
Decile Group	Net Income per Acre of Decile (Rs.)	Cumulative Percentage of Net Income	Net Income per Acre of Decile (Rs.)	Cumulative Percentage of Net Income
I	12,670.63	5.05	7,072.13	6.06
II	17,698.65	12.11	8,999.25	13.77
III	20,066.13	20.11	10,191.69	22.50
IV	22,206.73	30.56	10,869.75	31.82
V	24,065.15	38.57	11,440.82	41.62
VI	26,181.45	49.01	11,971.71	51.87
VII	28,255.80	60.28	12,678.56	62.74
VIII	29,859.86	72.18	13,255.47	74.07
IX	32,726.63	85.24	14,001.16	86.06
X	37,020.59	100.00	16,263.67	100.00
Gini Coefficients		0.159		0.121

In the case of CO 37 variety, 30 per cent (decile group I-III) of the bottom income earners received only 22.50 per cent of the total net income and 60 per cent (decile group I-VI) of them enjoyed about 52 per cent of it. The remaining 40 per cent (decile group VII-X) of the high income earners shared nearly half of the total net income. The 20 per cent (decile group IX-X) of the top income earners received more than quarter (25.95%) the total net income. Thus, while about half of the total net income was enjoyed by 40 per cent of the top income group, the rest of the amount was shared by the remaining 60 per cent of the farmers.

The Gini coefficient of distribution of net income was 0.159 for IR 20 variety and 0.121 for CO 37. It may be inferred that inequality in income distribution existed under both the rice varieties. Hence, the hypothesis of income inequality among the growers of the two rice varieties is accepted. However, the inequality in income distribution was greater under IR 20 than under CO 37 variety. The Lorenz curves corresponding to the net income distribution from IR 20 and CO 37 rice cultivation are given in Fig. 6.2.

In the figure, as the Lorenz curve of net income per acre for CO 37 variety lies closer to the diagonal and is above the IR 20 curve throughout, it may be inferred that there is a greater equality in the income distribution from the former than from the latter variety. Since the two curves lie very close to each other, it is to be tested statistically.

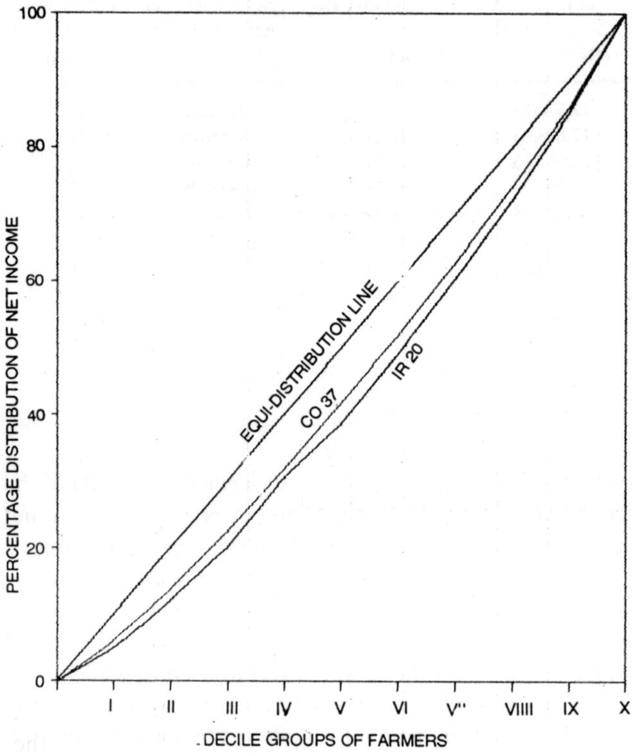

FIG. 6.2: Lorenz Curves of net Income Distribution per acre for IR 20 and CO 37 Varieties of Rice in Rabi Season, 1985-86

In the literature, there are no statistical tests available to compare the Gini concentration indexes. However, the variances of the logarithms of the variables can be considered as a measure of inequality,[10] for which statistical tests are available to observe the significance of difference between two variances of the logarithms of variables. In the study, the variances of the logarithms of the variables were calculated by using the formula:

$$\frac{1}{N}\sum_{i=1}^{N}(\log Z_i - \log \overline{Z})^2 = \frac{1}{N}\sum_{i=1}^{N}\left(\log \frac{Z_i}{\overline{Z}}\right)^2$$

where,

Z_i = income of the ith individual,
$\overline{Z}$ = mean income of all individuals, and
N = total sample size.

Assuming the variable to be log-normally distributed with mean λ and variances σ_1^2 and σ_2^2, the differences between σ_1^2 and σ_2^2 were tested using the F-ratio σ_1^2/σ_2^2.[11]

A comparison of the Gini concentration indexes using the variances of the logarithms of IR 20 (σ_1^2) and CO 37 (σ_2^2) worked out to be 0.021 and 0.015, respectively. As the calculated F-value 1.40 was less than the tabulated F-value 1.54 for (100,50) degrees of freedom at five per cent level, it could be concluded that there was no difference between the variances of the logarithms of IR 20 and CO 37 net income. In other words, no significant difference between the degree of inequality existed between the two varieties of rice.

In brief, income inequality was observed under both IR 20 and CO 37 varieties of rice in Gokilapuram, during rabi 1985-86. The Gini coefficients indicated relatively greater inequality in the net income distribution of IR 20 variety compared to CO 37. However, the statistical test indicated that no significant difference between the degree of inequality existed with respect to the two varieties of rice.

NOTES

1. A.K. Sen, "An Aspect of Indian Agriculture", *Economic Weekly*, Annual Number, Vol.XIV, Nos. 4, 5 & 6, February 1962.
2. M. Chattopadhyay and Ashok Rudra, "Size-Productivity Revisited", *Economic and Political Weekly*, Vol.XI, No. 39, September 25, 1976, pp. A-104—A-116.
3. G.R. Saini, "Holding Size, Productivity and Some Related Aspects of Indian Agriculture", *Economic and Political Weekly*, Vol.VI, No. 26, June 26, 1971, pp. A-79—A-85.
4. C.H. Hanumantha Rao, "Farm Size and the Distribution of Gains", *Technological Change and Distribution of Gains in Indian Agriculture*,

Macmillan Company of India Ltd., Delhi, 1975, pp. 75-88.

5. Madhusudan Ghosh, "Farm Size Productivity Nexus under Alternative Technology", *Indian Journal of Agricultural Economics*, Vol. 41, No.1, January-March 1986, pp. 17-28.
6. Hanumantha Rao, loc. cit.
7. Ghosh, loc. cit.
8. K.R. Ranadive, "Preface", *Income Distribution: The Unsolved Puzzle*, Oxford University Press, Bombay, 1978, pp. vii-viii.
9. C.J. Bliss and N.H. Stern, "Output and Income", *Palanpur: The Economy of an Indian Village*, Oxford University Press, Delhi, 1982, pp. 207-208.
10. H. Theil, *Economics and Information Theory*, North Holland Publishing Company, Amsterdam, 1967, pp. 121-125.
11. K. Kalirajan, "Benefits from the High-Yielding Varieties Programme and Their Distribution in an Irrigated Paddy Area", *Indian Journal of Agricultural Economics*, Vol.35, No.3, July-September 1980, pp. 73-74.

7

SUPPLY AND DEMAND ELASTICITIES, AND LABOUR ABSORPTION IN RICE CULTIVATION

In a country like India where agriculture occupies a strategic position, the analysis of agricultural production assumes an important role in the the formulation of agricultural policy, which forms an integral part of development policy. The main objective of agricultural policy is often the identification of possibilities for increasing output, while conserving the available resources. It includes aspects like price responsiveness, economics of scale, efficiency in the allocation of variable factors of production, shadow pricing of the fixed factors of production and relative efficiency. These aspects can be analysed using various econometric tools, of which, profit function is one.

In the conventional approach, supply response using time-series data is studied by regressing the quantity supplied on price, allowing for the lags and shifts in it. However, input demand and output supply being interlinked parts of a general system, estimation of output supply alone may give inefficient estimates of the underlying supply relationship. Lim[1] had reviewed the estimation difficulties involved in this approach. To avoid such problems, simultaneous estimation of output supply and factor demand equations become desirable. The profit function approach popularised by Lau and Yotopoulos[2] helps to derive output supply and factor demand equations. It expresses a farm's profit in terms of output price, prices of variable factors and quantities of fixed factors of production. Thus, it adopts a more realistic approach by accounting for the fact that resource endowments, prices and technology may vary from farmer to farmer.

Profit function is a tool for the analysis of the determinants of agricultural production. Due to its flexibility in use arising out of the duality between profit function and production function, it is being widely used for the study of production. In the profit function approach, real profit is expressed as a function of real prices of variable inputs and quantities of fixed factors of production.

Although production function and profit function are in neo-classical frame, they differ from each other in their approaches.[3] In the production function approach:

(i) Quantity of output is the dependent and quantities of factors of production are the independent variables.
(ii) Profit maximisation is assumed.
(iii) Based on the profit maximisation assumption, demand function and supply function are derived by solving an optimisation problem.

In the profit function approach:

(i) The normalised restricted profit function is estimated as a function of the prices of variable inputs and quantities of fixed inputs;
(ii) Profit maximisation is assumed;
(iii) The demand function and supply function are directly derived from the normalised profit function; and
(iv) This approach gives statistically consistent estimates under standard assumptions, while the traditional production function (solved, using the ordinary least squares estimator) may be subject to simultaneous equation bias and give inconsistent estimates.

The profit function approach suffers from certain limitations such as it is a static model; it uses actual profits as a proxy for expected profits; the assumption of profit maximisation is unlikely to prevail in a risky environment when the farmer will only prefer to maximise utility. Despite these limitations, the advantages of using a profit function model based on competitive principles (Lau and Yotopoulos,[4] Subramaniyan[5] and Kalirajan and Shand[6]) are as follows:

(a) By partially differentiating the 'real' profit with respect to the real price of ith input, one can obtain a theoretically and economically efficient demand function for i^{th} input.
(b) The assumption of profit maximisation can be verified by jointly considering the variable factor demand functions and the profit function.
(c) The assumption of a competitive model explaining the market behaviour can be statistically verified by examining the

equality between the marginal product of ith input and its price.

(d) Own and cross price elasticities of other variable inputs can readily be obtained.

(e) Above all, the demand for input is not derived independently, but jointly as a system of output supply and factor demand equations which incorporates the inter-dependent nature of output and input decisions made by farmers.

The profit function is inherently a cross-sectional approach.[7] The price variables are the crucial factors in the estimation of cost and profit function. Absence of variations in the prices of factors used in the study may render the estimation of profit function impossible. In other words, application of a profit function approach is warranted only under the conditions of price variations between farms at a point of time. Therefore, the coefficient of variations in prices of the variables used in this study were computed for IR 20 and CO 37 rice varieties, which are reported in Table 7.1.

TABLE 7.1: Price Variations in the Variables of IR 20 and CO 37 Rice

Variables	Coefficient of Variation (in Percentage)	
	IR 20	CO 37
1. Wage Rate	9.92	15.55
2. Fertilizer Price	11.44	19.93
3. Pesticides Price	55.21	66.50
4. Bullock Pair Price	11.27	10.21
5. Output per Acre	9.93	10.58

The coefficient of variation among the variables for the two varieties ranged from about 10 per cent to more than 66 per cent. The reported price variability was the highest for pesticides. This may be attributed to the heterogeneous range of the input. The variation in fertilizer price was 11 to 20 per cent. Fertilizer being a standard product, price variability in it may be due to transport cost and variations in dealer prices. The coefficient of variations for bullock pair, wage rate and output per acre were below 16 per cent. However, these price variations do not indicate the absence of a competitive market in the study area or that there were major obstacles in the functioning of factor and product markets. According to Kalirajan,[8] "the differences in rice and input prices between farmers were largely due to the differences in transport costs to market and to some extent by price movements brought about by the seasonality of demand and supply for goods and services".

As sufficient price variations were observed in the cross-section data of the variables used, the profit function analysis has been adopted in the study. Initiality, the trans-log profit function (which is more flexible than the Cobb-Douglas profit function) was tried and then dropped, as the coefficients of cross-product terms and square terms were insignificant in most of the cases owing to high correlations. Consequently, the matrix became singular. Hence, the Cobb-Douglas form of profit function was adopted mainly for two reasons: (i) estimation of parameters is straight-forward as is their interpretation in the dual profit function, which is also Cobb-Douglas, and (ii) using this model facilitates ready comparison of the results with those of the others.

The normalised profit function corresponding to Cobb-Douglas production function was jointly estimated along with the four variable input demand functions with random disturbances. It was of the form:

$$\log \pi^* = \alpha_0 + \beta_1^* \log W + \beta_2^* \log F + \beta_3^* \log P + \beta_4^* \log B + \alpha_1^* \log A + \alpha_2^* \log C + U \quad (1)$$

$$\frac{-WX_1}{\pi^*} = \beta_1^* + U_1$$

$$\frac{-FX_2}{\pi^*} = \beta_2^* + U_2 \quad (2)$$

$$\frac{-PX_3}{\pi^*} = \beta_3^* + U_3$$

$$\frac{-BX_4}{\pi^*} = \beta_4^* + U_4$$

π^* = real profit in rupees (i.e., total revenue minus total variable cost normalised by the price of output)

W = real wages for labour,

F = real fertilizer price,

P = real pesticides price,

B real bullock pair day price,

A = total area cultivated,

C = capital flow (calculated as the sum of depreciation, maintenance and opportunity cost of capital stock).
X_1 = total labour mandays utilised,
X_2 = total quantity of fertilizers used,
X_3 = total quantity of pesticides used,
X_4 = total bullock pair days, and
U = random disturbances.

The equations (1) and (2) were jointly estimated using Zellner's seemingly unrelated regression which give asymptotically more efficient estimates than the production function estimated by the ordinary least squares method.[9] Table 7.2 presents the results for IR 20 and CO 37 rice varieties.

TABLE 7.2: Normalised Profit Function and Factor Demand Elasticities for IR 20 and CO 37 Rice Varieties

Variables	Parameters	Restricted Estimates	
		IR 20	CO 37
Profit Function Constant	α_0	7.6329	7.6222
Log *W*	β_1^{*0}	−0.3323*	−2.2769*
		(−8.7088)	(−60.4824)
Log *F*	β_2^*	−0.1215*	0.0615
		(−9.0856)	(1.1024)
Log *P*	β_3^*	−0.0250*	−0.0295*
		(−0.6556)	(−0.6651)
Log *B*	β_4^*	−0.0390*	−0.0242*
		(−10.3574)	(−22.8811)
Log *A*	α_1^*	0.9489*	0.9845*
		(31.3984)	(26.5006)
Log *C*	α_2^*	0.0552	0.0147
		(1.9462)	(0.3444)
Labour Demand	β_1^*	−0.3323*	−0.2770*
		(−8.9883)	(−64.5643)
Fertilizer Demand	β_2^*	−0.1215*	0.0615
		(−9.3772)	(1.1768)
Pesticides Demand	β_3^*	−0.0250*	−0.0295*
		(−9.9655)	(−10.3174)
Bullock Labour Demand	β_4^*	−0.0390*	−0.0242*
		(−10.6898)	(−24.4253)

Note: Figures in parentheses represent *t*-value.
*Indicates significance at 5 per cent level.

7.1 Labour Demand and Supply Response

Along with increased production, the introduction of the new agricultural technology was also expected to increase employment opportunities in the sector. Labour requirement in agriculture is basically determined by the type of technology used, distribution of land ownership, and social, economic, institutional and political conditions. Labour absorption and the technology suited for it is still a controversial issue in Indian agriculture. In view of the mounting unemployment and disguised unemployment in the sector, the conventional approach favours the adoption of labour-intensive technology (Khusro,[10] Mehra,[11] Rudra and Mukhopadyay[12]) rather than the modern capital-intensive technology. Some of the empirical studies by Johl,[13] Subramaniyan,[14] Bisaliah[15] and Sharma[16] for India have revealed that the new technology has succeeded in off-setting the labour-saving effects of mechanisation through the adoption of High Yielding Varieties (HYV), multiple cropping and intensive usage of factor inputs. Nevertheless, the influence of the existing agrarian structure, labour market and the socio-political aspects should not be overlooked. Amidst the prevailing debates, an examination of the labour-absorptive capacity of IR 20 and CO 37 HYV rice in Gokilapuram village assumes vital importance in the formulation of agricultural policy.

Further, the success or failure of government intervention in increasing production and farmers' welfare depends on the responses of farm households to input and output price changes. An evaluation of the efficacy of market instruments (prices), for example, involves the estimation of demand and supply functions from which one may study the responsiveness of agricultural producers to changes in market prices. Governments typically use a combination of short-run price policies and long-run instruments (investment in technology and infrastructure) to achieve their objectives, so as to increase output and farm incomes. Under the circumstances of rising input costs against the output prices, a study on the rice supply responses and input demand to changing prices among the farmers becomes imperative. The elasticities obtained from such an analysis would contribute important information towards the formulation of agricultural policy. This section of the chapter highlights the supply responsiveness of rice and demand for inputs with regard to their own prices and the prices of other inputs.

Given the profit function estimates, own and cross price elasticities of demand for factor inputs and supply elasticities of rice were calculated using the formula given in Table 7.3.

TABLE 7.3: Formulae to Estimate Output Supply and Input Demand Elasticities from Cobb-Douglas Profit Function

Description	Parameters of Profit Function
(a) Supply Elasticities:	
(i) With respect to real price of ith variables input, X_i	β^*_i
(ii) With respect to fixed input, Z_j	α^*_j
(iii) With respect to output price, P_y	$-\Sigma\beta^*_i$
b) Input demand elasticities:	
(i) Own price elasticity of X_i	$\beta^*_i - 1$
(ii) Cross price elasticity for X_i with respect to real price P_j	β^*_i
(iii) Variable input X_i with respect to fixed factor Z_j	α^*_j
(iv) Demand elasticity of X_i with respect to output price	$-\Sigma\beta^*_i + 1$

Source: L.J. Lau and P.A. Yotopoulos, "Profit, Supply and Factor Demand Functions", *American Journal of Agricultural Economics,* Vol. 54, No. 1, February 1972, p. 17.

Table 7.4 reports the own and cross price elasticities of demand for labour and output supply of rice for IR 20 and CO 37 varieties in Gokilapuram.

TABLE 7.4: Own and Cross Price Elasticities of Demand for Labour and Output Supply for IR 20 and CO 37 Rice Varieties

Exogenous Variables	Endogenous Variables			
	Output Supply		Labour Demand	
	IR 20	CO 37	IR 20	CO 37
Rice Price	0.5178	0.2691	1.5178	1.2691
Real Wage	−0.3323	−0.2770	−1.3323	−1.2770
Real Fertilizer Price	−0.1215	0.0615	−0.1215	−0.0615
Real Pesticides Price	−0.0250	−0.0295	−0.0250	−0.0295
Real Bullock Pair Price	−0.0390	−0.0242	−0.0390	−0.0242
Land	0.9490	0.9845	0.9490	0.9845
Capital	0.0552	0.0147	0.0552	0.0147

The output supply elasticities for IR 20 and CO 37 rice varieties with respect to own prices were 0.5178 and 0.2691 respectively. In other words, ceteris paribus, a 10 per cent increase in rice price would respectively increase their output supply by 5.18 per cent and 2.69 per cent. This implied that the Gokilapuram farmers were not so responsive to changes in rice price in general. The finding supports Mellor's[17] hypothesis that output price does not have much effect on its supply. This indicates that manipulation of rice price may not be considered as an effective policy tool to increase output supply in the village. Since most of the government policy objectives aim at raising consumers' welfare in general, this result is encouraging from the national point of view. This result is in conformity with the findings of Tamin[18] and Somel[19] for rice (0.417) and wheat (0.521) respectively.

Changes in rice price appeared to have a significant effect on the demand for labour in rice cultivation. A 10 per cent increase in rice price was found to ensure a more than 10 per cent rise (15.18 per cent for IR 20 and 12.69 per cent for CO 37) in the demand for labour.

In both cases, an increase in the real prices of the variable inputs negatively affected rice supply and demand for labour, except in the case of fertilizer for CO 37. The magnitude of elasticities and hence the influence of these variables were quite low in the determination of output supply and labour demand in rice farming. However, increase in farm wage had a relatively serious negative effect on the supply of rice and demand for labour. The elasticities indicated that a 10 per cent increase in real wage would induce the sample farmers to reduce labour employment by 13.32 per cent in the case of IR 20 and 12.77 per cent for CO 37 rice. This implied that wage rate is also one of the factors that significantly affects farm employment.

The elasticities of rice output in relation to land were 0.95 and 0.98 for IR 20 and CO 37 rice respectively. In the case of capital, the respective elasticities were quite negligible (0.0552 and 0.0147). This indicated that an increase in area under rice had a favourable impact on rice supply compared to capital flows. These findings are almost similar to the results of Kalirajan and Shand[20] and Subramaniyan.[21]

The study shows that a modernised rice crop enterprise has the capacity to absorb an increased amount of labour. This may be done through price policy measures. A slight decrease in wage rate was observed to induce a greater employment of labour. But this may not be practicable due to the active labour unions which may resist any undue wage cuts. Therefore, the policy-makers can resort to output price policy, as an increase in rice price is observed to induce substantial labour absorption in the study area. However, output price policy should not be considered as the only solution to reduce agricultural unemployment. Improvement of non-economic factors like labour organisations, inheritance system and social structure, along with an incentive price policy can also have a salutary effect on labour employment in agriculture. However, the suitability of any policy should be judged in the light of its overall social and economic consequences.

Table 7.5 gives the demand for variable inputs with respect to their own prices for IR 20 and CO 37 rice varieties.

TABLE 7.5: Demand for Variable Inputs with respect to its Own Price for IR 20 and CO 37 Rice Varieties

Particulars	IR 20	CO 37
Demand for Labour with respect to Real Wage	−1.3323	−1.2770
Demand for Fertilizer with respect to Real Fertilizer Price	−1.1215	−0.9385
Demand for Pesticides with respect to Real Pesticides Price	−1.0250	−1.0295
Demand for Bullock Pair with respect to Real Bullock Pair Price	−1.0390	−1.0242

The analysis revealed that a 10 per cent increase in the prices of variable inputs, labour, fertilizer, pesticides and bullock labour was accompanied by 13.32 per cent, 11.22 per cent, 10.25 per cent and 10.39 per cent decrease in their respective demands in IR 20. In the case of CO 37, it was followed by a decline of 12.77 per cent, 0.94 per cent, 10.29 per cent and 10.24 per cent in the demands of the respective variable inputs. This indicated that the demands for variable inputs with respect to their own prices were highly elastic. That is, a 10 per cent increase in the prices of the variable inputs was followed by a more than 10 per cent fall in their demands. Adulavidhaya, et al.[22] and Subramaniyan[23] arrived at similar conclusions in their studies.

Among the prices of variable inputs, real wage appeared to be relatively the most important factor of production affecting the agricultural employment to a considerable extent.

The own and cross price elasticities of demand for variable inputs with respect to IR 20 and CO 37 varieties of rice are presented in Table 7.6.

TABLE 7.6: Own and Cross Price Elasticities of Demand for Variable Inputs for IR 20 and CO 37 Rice Varieties

Particulars	Price of Labour	Price of Fertilizer	Price of Pesticides	Price of Bullock Pair
	IR 20			
Demand for Labour	−1.3323	−0.1215	−0.0250	−0.0390
Demand for Fertilizer	−0.3323	−1.1215	−0.0250	−0.0390
Demand for Pesticides	−0.3323	−0.1215	−1.0250	−0.0390
Demand for Bullock Pair	−0.3323	−0.1215	−0.0250	−1.0390
	CO 37			
Demand for Labour	−1.2770	0.0615	−0.0295	−0.0242
Demand for Fertilizer	−0.2770	−0.9385	−0.0295	−0.0242
Demand for Pesticides	−0.2770	0.0615	−1.0295	−0.0242
Demand for Bullock Pair	−0.2770	0.0615	−0.0295	−1.0242

The Table 7.6 shows that the cross price elasticities of the variable inputs for IR 20 variety were negative and low, indicating that they were complements rather than substitutes. Similarly for CO 37 variety, the cross price elasticities emerged negative and low for all inputs, except fertilizer. The positive sign of cross price elasticity of fertilizer implied that the factors were substitutes. The CO 37 rice being a locally bred high-yielding variety, it may be possible for fertilizer and pesticides to be substitutes. But, this does not sound logical in the cases of human labour and bullock labour, as they cannot be substituted by fertilizer. However, as the magnitudes of their cross-elasticities were quite low, they can be ignored. Further, it may be noted that a given change in any of the exogeneous variable in inputs demand is symmetric in this approach, which is due to the inherent assumption of unit elasticity of substitution among input pairs in the Cobb-Douglas production function.

In sum, although the cross price elasticities among the variable inputs were low, indicating a weak relationship, these factors were observed to be complements rather than substitutes of each other. Lau, Lin and Yotopoulos,[24] Tamin[25] and Adulavidhaya, et al.[26] reported almost similar findings.

7.2 Direct and Indirect Production Elasticities

One of the advantages of the profit function approach is that from the estimated elasticities of real profit function, indirect estimates of the production elasticities may be derived. These estimates are consistent estimates of the production function elasticities and are called indirect estimates, to distinguish them from the direct estimates, which are obtained by estimating the production function directly.[27] However, the indirect estimates of the production elasticities are not strictly comparable to the direct estimates of the production elasticities. The direct estimates derived from the conventional Cobb-Douglas production function are obtained by the single equation ordinary least squares method. Therefore, these estimates are subject to simultaneous equations bias. The indirect estimates are free from such bias as they are obtained through the simultaneous solution of the profit and factor demand functions. Given the stochastic assumptions, these estimates are statistically consistent and asymptotically efficient. Further, the stochastic specification and the definition of the variables in the production and profit functions are different.

Using the parameter estimates of the normalised profit function, the indirect estimates of production elasticities were computed using the following formula given by Lau and Yotopoulos:[28]

$$\alpha_j = \alpha_j^* (1 - \mu^*)^{-1}; \qquad j = 1, 2, \cdots m$$

$$\beta_j = -\beta_j^* (1 - \mu^*)^{-1}; \qquad j = 1, 2, \cdots n$$

$$\mu^* = \sum_{j=1}^{n} \beta_j^*$$

where,

α_i = indirect estimates of production elasticities of the fixed inputs,

β_j = indirect estimates of production elasticities of the variable inputs,

α_j^* = coefficients of fixed inputs in the profit function, and

β_j^* = coefficients of variable inputs in the profit functions.

In order to obtain the direct production elasticities, Cobb-Douglas production function was estimated with yield as the dependent variable and labour, fertilizer, pesticides, bullock labour, land and capital as the independent variables.

The direct and indirect production elasticities are listed in Table 7.7.

TABLE 7.7: Direct and Indirect Estimates of Production Elasticities

Variables	IR 20		CO 37	
	Direct	Indirect	Direct	Indirect
Labour	0.36*	0.22	0.26*	0.22
	(6.63)		(3.57)	
Fertilizer	0.30*	0.08	–0.001	–0.05
	(5.36)		(–0.030)	
Pesticides	0.04*	0.02	0.39*	0.02
	(2.03)		(8.90)	
Bullock Pair	0.24*	0.03	0.14*	0.02
	(4.93)		(2.33)	
Area	0.08*	0.63	0.22*	0.78
	(3.06)		(2.95)	
Capital	0.06*	0.04	0.02	0.01
	(2.42)		(0.96)	
Sum of Elasticities	1.08	1.02	1.03	1.00
$\bar{R}^2$	0.97		0.98	

Notes: Estimated as described by Yotopoulos and Lau, 1979, p. 21.
Figures in parentheses represent *t*-value.
*Indicates significance at 5 per cent level.

The indirect estimates are preferable over direct estimates because the latter is subject to simultaneous equation bias. It is not possible to test whether the two estimates of the production elasticities are significantly different, as the indirect estimates do not have standard error. Therefore, only the indirect estimates for the two varieties are discussed here.

The magnitude of the indirect estimates of the production function elasticities seemed to be quite logical and consistent with the a priori expectations of economic theory. The notable feature was the dominance of the production elasticity of land with 0.63 for IR 20 and 0.78 for CO 37 rice. In both cases, labour was the next important factor with an elasticity of 0.22 each. This highlighted the importance of land and labour as factors of production, with the respective share of more than 60 per cent and 22 per cent in the total output of the two varieties. It was followed by fertilizer for IR 20 rice (0.08), while its value was negative and low for CO 37 variety. This may be because the former variety is more fertilizer responsive than the latter.[29] The production elasticity of pesticides was 0.02 for both varieties of rice. This result is in conformity with the findings of Flinn, Kalirajan and Castillo.[30] They attributed this behaviour to the characteristics of the modern varieties grown, which are resistant to many of the common pests. Bullock pair and capital did not figure prominently in the two varieties.

The indirect estimates for the two varieties revealed the prevalence of constant returns to scale. This finding rules out the policy of consolidation of holdings in the study area. Kalirajan and Flinn[31] also identified constant returns to scale in rice cultivation.

In brief, the indirect estimates indicated the dominance of land and labour as the important factors of production with respect to both IR 20 and CO 37 varieties of rice. This result is supported by the findings of Tamin[32] and Subramaniyan.[33] The shares of other factors did not figure prominently in total output. There was constant return to scale in both cases, implying consolidation of holdings does not seem relevant in Gokilapuram.

NOTES

1. D. Lim, *Supply Responses of Primary Producers,* Penerbit University, Malaya, Kuala Lumpur, 1975.
2. Lawrence J. Lau and Pan A. Yotopoulos, "Profits, Supply and Factor Demand Functions", *American Journal of Agricultural Economics,* Vol. 54, No. 1, February 1972, pp. 11-18.
3. P.A. Yotopoulos and L.J. Lau (Eds.), *Resource Use in Agriculture: Application of Profit Function to Selected Countries,* Food Research Institute Studies, Vol.

XVII, No. 2, 1979, p. 2.

4. Lau and Yotopoulos, loc. cit.
5. G. Subramaniyan, *Cotton in Madurai District: An Econometric Analysis,* Northern Book Centre, New Delhi, 1987, pp. 118-119.
6. K. Kalirajan and R.T. Shand, "Labour Absorption in Tamil Nadu Agriculture: A Micro Analysis", *Developing Economies,* Vol. XX, No. 3, September 1981, pp. 333-343.
7. John Quiggin and Anh Bui-Lan, "The use of Cross-Sectional Estimates of Profit Functions for Tests of Relative Efficiency: A Critical Review", *Australian Journal of Agricultural Economics,* Vol. 28, No. 1, April 1984, pp. 44-55.
8. K. Kalirajan and J.C. Flinn, "Allocative Efficiency and Supply Response in Irrigated Rice Production", *Indian Journal of Agricultural Economics,* Vol. 36, No. 2, April-June 1981, pp. 16-24.
9. Arnold Zellner, "An Efficient Method for Estimating Seemingly-Unrelated Regressions and Tests of Aggregation Bias", *Journal of the American Statistical Association,* Vol. 57, No. 2, June 1962, pp. 348-375.
10. A.M. Khusro, "Returns to Scale in Indian Agriculture", *Indian Journal of Agricultural Economics,* Vol. XIX, Nos. 3 & 4, July-December 1964, pp. 51-80.
11. S. Mehra, "Some Aspects of Labour Use in Indian Agriculture", *Indian Journal of Agricultural Economics,* Vol. 31, No. 4, October-December 1976, pp. 95-125.
12. A. Rudra and M.M. Mukhopadyay, "Hiring of Labour by Poor Peasants", *Economic and Political Weekly,* Vol. 11, Nos. 1 & 2, 10th January 1976, pp. 33-36.
13. S.S. Johl, *Mechanization, Labour Use and Productivity in Indian Agriculture,* Ohio State University, U.S.A., 1974.
14. Subramaniyan, loc. cit.
15. S. Bisaliah, "Decomposition Analysis of Employment Change under New Production Technology in Punjab Agriculture", *Indian Journal of Agricultural Economics,* Vol. 33, No. 2, April-June 1978, pp. 70-80.
16. R.K. Sharma, "Green Revolution and Farm Employment: An Analysis of Experience in Punjab", *Indian Journal of Industrial Relations,* Vol. 10, No. 2, October 1974.
17. J.W. Mellor, "Determinants of Rural Poverty: The Dynamics of Production, Technology and Prices", *Agricultural Change and Rural Poverty* (Eds.), J.W. Mellor and G.M. Desai, Food Policy Research Institute, Washington, D.C., 1985, pp. 21-40.
18. Mokhtar Tamin, "Micro Economic Analysis of Production Behaviour of Malaysian Farms: Lessons from MUDA" (Eds.), Yotopoulos and Lau, op. cit., pp. 87-98.
19. Kutlu Somel, "Technological Changes in Dryland Wheat Production in Turkey", Ibid., pp. 51-65.
20. Kalirajan and Shand, loc. cit.
21. G. Subramaniyan, "Labour Demand and Supply Responsiveness of Cotton in Madurai District", *Indian Journal of Agricultural Economics,* Vol. 41, No.2. April-June 1986, pp. 155-163.
22. Kamphol Adulavidhaya, et al., "A Micro Economic Analysis of the Agriculture of Thailand" (Eds.), Yotopoulos and Lau, op. cit., pp. 79-86.
23. Subramaniyan, loc. cit.
24. L.J. Lau, Wuu-Long Lin and P.A. Yotopoulos, "Efficiency and Technology

Change in Taiwan" (Eds.), Yotopoulos and Lau, op. cit., pp. 23-50.

25. Tamin, loc. cit.
26. Adulavidhaya, et al., loc. cit.
27. Lau, Lin and Yotopoulos, op.cit., p. 41.
28. Lau and Yotopoulos, loc. cit.,
29. R.N. Poduval, "Adoption of New Technology", *Foodgrains Economy of Tamil Nadu: Problems and Prospects,* Emerald Publishers, Madras, 1987, p. 32.
30. J.C. Flinn, K. Kalirajan and Linda L. Castillo, "Supply Responsiveness of Rice Farmers in Laguna, Philippines", *Australian Journal of Agricultural Economics,* Vol. 26, No. 1, April 1982, pp. 39-48.
31. Kalirajan and Flinn, loc. cit.
32. Tamin, loc. cit.
33. Subramaniyan, loc. cit.

8

ECONOMIC EFFICIENCY

The concept of economic efficiency is one of the most important criteria for evaluating decision-making in the production process. It seeks to measure the outcome of specific objectives in relation to the efforts made to achieve it. The efforts made in agriculture relate to the use and allocation of scarce resources among alternative uses, with the objective of maximising profits. Profit maximisation is the crux of the economic theory of production. A study of efficiency assumes importance in a developing country like India, due to its diversified farming system and varied soil type, size of holding, technology adopted, resource constraints, etc.

Since the introduction of the new agrarian technology, the study of economic efficiency has gained importance in economic analysis. Economic efficiency constitutes price or allocative efficiency and technical efficiency. While the former is a behavioural concept, the latter is an engineering concept. A farm may be said to be price efficient if it maximises profits from a given set of inputs by equating the marginal value product with marginal cost of the factors of production. It tests whether two farmer groups are able to realise the expected profits to the same degree by adjusting the variable factors of production, given their prices. On the other hand, a farm may be said to be technically efficient if it consistently produces larger quantities of output from a given set of inputs. Differences in economic efficiency may result from differences in technical/price efficiencies. A production function approach does not permit a study on price efficiency as it does not incorporate prices as exogeneous variables, nor does it account for the different factor endowments between farms. These limitations are well taken care of in the profit function analysis.

Two identical farms that have attained maximum profits can still have earned different amounts due to the different effective prices they face. The profit function approach is able to accommodate these price differences and study technical and price efficiencies by incorporating price as pre-determined variable. Thus, it can explain adequately the production behaviour of farmers. It facilitates a comparative economic evaluation of the new technology by studying all three components of efficiency.

An analysis of economic efficiency is vital to policy-makers in framing policies relating to land reforms both at the micro and macro levels. Further, the analysis of technical and price efficiencies provides useful information for policy making on agricultural education and extension policies.

There are different views on the economic efficiency of farmer groups in Indian agriculture. Numerous studies have been conducted on the basis of production function. However, studies based on profit function to examine the efficiency of farmer groups in the context of Indian agriculture is very limited. The present study explores into the relative economic efficiency of farmer groups, within the framework of profit function analysis. As the number of farmers growing CO 37 was limited, the classification of sample farmers into small and large farmer groups was not possible. Hence, this study is restricted only to the relative economic efficiency of IR 20 rice farmers in Gokilapuram during rabi season, 1985-86. The purpose is to examine the impact of the new technology on the relative economic efficiency of the farmers cultivating IR 20 rice. It deals with the production efficiency of how well the farms in different categories of size convert inputs into output.

The primary objectives of this study are:

(i) to examine the relative economic efficiency of the farmer groups growing IR 20 variety of rice, and

(ii) to identify the sources of difference in economic efficiency, if any, between small and large farmer groups growing IR 20 rice.

In this context, the following hypotheses have been tested:

(i) small farmers and large farmers are equally economic efficient,

(ii) small farmers and large farmers are equally price efficient, and

(iii) small farmers and large farmers are equally technical efficient.

To pursue the above objectives and to test the related hypotheses, the Cobb-Douglas profit function along with the four variable input demand equations of the following form were jointly estimated:

$$\log \pi^* = \lambda + \alpha_0^* D_1 + \beta_1^* \log W + \beta_2^* \log F + \beta_3^* \log P$$
$$+ \beta_4^* \log B + \alpha_1^* \log A + \alpha_2^* \log C + U \quad (1)$$

$$\frac{-WX_1}{\pi^*} = \beta_1^{*L} D_1 + \beta_1^{*S} D_2 + V_1$$

$$\frac{-FX_2}{\pi^*} = \beta_2^{*L} D_1 + \beta_2^{*S} D_2 + V_2 \quad (2)$$

$$\frac{-PX_3}{\pi^*} = \beta_3^{*L} D_1 + \beta_3^{*S} D_2 + V_3$$

$$\frac{-BX_4}{\pi^*} = \beta_4^{*L} D_1 + \beta_4^{*S} D_2 + V_4$$

where,

π^*	=	unit output price (UOP) profit in rupees,
W	=	normalised wage rate for labour,
F	=	normalised fertilizer price,
P	=	normalised pesticides price,
B	=	normalised bullock pair price per day,
A	=	total area cultivated,
C	=	capital flow (calculated as the sum of depreciation, maintenance and opportunity cost of capital stock),
X_1	=	total labour mandays utilized,
X_2	=	total quantity of fertilizer used,
X_3	=	total quantity of pesticides used,
X_4	=	total bullock pair days employed,
U	=	random disturbances,
V	=	represents divergence between expected and realised price and statistical errors,
λ	=	constant,
D_1	=	one for large farmer group and zero otherwise,
D_2	=	one for small farmer group and zero otherwise,
L	=	large farmer group, and
S	=	small farmer group.

8.1 Test for Relative Economic Efficiency

The test of equal relative economic efficiency between the farmer groups requires that the parameters of the profit function and factor demand function should be the same for small and large farmers. In other words, the dummy variable coefficient, α_0^*, must be zero in (1). It may be represented as:

$$H_N: a_0^* = O$$

8.2 Test for Equal Price Efficiency

The test of equal relative price efficiency between the farmer groups requires that the two groups of farmers equate marginal value product of each factor to its marginal cost, to the same degree. That is, the elasticities of variable inputs of small farmers (β_i^{*S}) and large farmers (β_i^{*L}) estimated from the factor demand equation should coincide with each other. It may be represented as:

$$H_N : \beta_i^{*L} = \beta_i^{*S}, \quad i = 1, 2, 3, 4.$$

where,

L = large farmers; and
S = small farmers.

8.3 Test for Equal Price and Technical Efficiency

The test of equal relative technical efficiency between the farmer groups involves the joint testing of the hypotheses of equal relative economic efficiency and price efficiency. It may be represented as:

$$H_N : \alpha_0^{*} = 0; \quad \text{and} \quad \beta_i^{*L} = \beta_i^{*S}, \quad i = 1, 2, 3, 4.$$

The above restrictions were incorporated into the model by using Zellner's seemingly unrelated regressions,[1] as it is an asymptotically more efficient method of estimation. Both restricted and unrestricted estimates of the analysis are presented in Table 8.1 for IR 20 farmer groups.

The Table 8.1 reveals the coefficient of dummy variable (α_0^{i}) to be negative and statistically significant at five per cent level. This indicates that there was no evidence to accept the null hypothesis that both small farms and large farms are equally efficient. More specifically, small farmers were economically more efficient than large farmers in Gokilapuram. This may be due to the more intensive use of factors of production by them. Added to it, is the advantage of relatively smaller size of their operational holdings which enable better personal supervision and farm management. Lau and Yotopoulos[2] and Dutta[3] arrived at similar conclusion in the context of Indian farms. On the other hand, Hanumantha Rao,[4] Subramaniyan[5] and Khan and Maki[6] found large farmers to be economically more efficient than small farmers. Still other studies (Kalirajan,[7] Rajagopalan,[8] Kalirajan[9] and Parthasarthy and Prasad[10]) reported the small and large rice farmers to be equally economically efficient.

TABLE 8.1: Joint Estimation of Cobb-Douglas Profit Function and Input Demand Equations for IR 20 Rice

Variables	Parameters	Unrestricted	Restricted
Profit Function Constant	λ	6.7425*	7.6329*
		(9.0969)	(49.0655)
Normalised Wage	β_1^*	0.4860	−0.3323*
		(1.5238)	(−8.7088)
Normalised Fertilizer Price	β_2^*	−0.0883	−0.1215*
		(−0.3198)	(−9.0856)
Normalised Pesticides Price	β_3^*	0.0038	−0.0250*
		(0.0576)	(−9.6556)
Normalised Animal Power Price	β_4^*	−0.3729	−0.0390*
		(−1.3284)	(−10.3574)
Land	α_1^*	1.0398*	0.9490*
		(12.7182)	(31.3984)
Capital	α_2^*	0.0864	0.0552
		(1.1437)	(1.9462)
D_1	α_0^*	−0.4523*	−0.1601*
		(−2.7386)	(−2.6669)
Labour Share Function	β_1^{*L}	−0.4024	−0.3323*
		(−8.5476)	(−8.9883)
	β_1^{*S}	−0.5423*	−0.3323*
		(−6.8276)	(−8.9883)
Fertilizer Share Function	β_2^{*L}	−0.1396*	−0.1215*
		(−8.5368)	(−9.3772)
	β_2^{*S}	−0.2039*	−0.1215*
		(−7.3893)	(−9.3772)
Pesticides Share Function	β_3^{*L}	−0.0307*	−0.0250*
		(−9.9114)	(−9.9665)
	β_3^{*S}	−0.0300*	−0.0250*
		(−5.7456)	(−9.9665)
Animal Power Share Function	β_4^{*L}	−0.0445*	−0.0390*
		(−9.6945)	(−10.6898)
	β_4^{*S}	−0.0604*	−0.0390*
		(−7.8047)	(−10.6898)

Note: Figures in parentheses represent *t*-value.
* Indicates significance at 5 per cent level.

Further, in order to identify the sources of difference in economic efficiency of the IR 20 farmer groups, F-tests were used. The analysis was based on restricted estimates. The results of the tests are presented in Table 8.2.

TABLE 8.2: Tests of Economic Efficiency between Small and Large IR 20 Rice Farmers in Gokilapuram, Rabi 1985-86

Hypothesis Tested	Computed F-Value	Degrees of Freedom	Inference
1. Test for Equal Relative Economic Efficiency			
$H_N : \alpha_0^* = 0$	5.59	(1,484)	$\alpha_0^* \neq 0$; Difference
2. Test for Equal Relative Price Efficiency:			
(a) *By inputs:*			
Labour	2.42	(1,484)	No difference
Fertilizer	4.23	(1,484)	Difference
Pesticides	0.01	(1,484)	No difference
Bullock pair	3.30	(1,484)	No difference
(b) For over-all inputs	2.58	(4,484)	Significant difference at 5% level
3. Test for Equal Technical Efficiency	2.50	(5,484)	Small farms are technically more efficient
$H_N : \alpha_0^* = 0$: and $\beta_i^{*L} = \beta_i^{*S}$; $i = 1, 2, 3, 4$.			

Note: Critical values are:
$F_{.05}(1, \alpha) = 3.84$;
$F_{.05}(4, \alpha) = 2.37$;
$F_{.05}(5, \alpha) = 2.21$.

The null hypothesis of equal economic efficiency between small and large farmers was rejected. This indicated that the test of relative economic efficiency was in favour of the small farms. In other words, given the fixed inputs (land and fixed capital) and within the ranges of the observed prices of output and variable inputs, small farms of the sample studied had higher actual profits in Gokilapuram.

The test of equal relative price efficiency of farmer groups by inputs revealed that the two groups were equally price efficient with regard to labour, pesticides and bullock pair day. However, they were not equally price efficient with respect to fertilizer. Considering all inputs together, the test showed that the two farmer groups were not equally price efficient. This implied that both groups did not succeed in maximising profits to the same degree, in the study area.

The test of equal price and technical efficiency showed that the hypothesis of equal relative technical efficiency could be rejected at five per cent level of significance. Small farmers emerged technically more efficient than the large farmers. This may be due to better farm management favoured by the smaller size of their operational holdings.

In sum, small farmers were found to be economically more efficient in Gokilapuram, during the rabi season 1985-86. The two farmer groups were equally price efficient with regard to all variable inputs, except fertilizer. This may be due to uncertainty which may be one of the reasons for applying fertilizer less than the profit maximising choices. This difference was significant at five per cent level. Small farmers were technically more efficient than the large farmers. This may be due to the inverse proportional relationship between farm size and productivity. These findings indicate that in agriculture, direct supervision and leadership role of the owner-manager may be crucial for attaining high levels of economic efficiency. However, more studies are in fact necessary to explore into the factors causing the difference in economic efficiency of farmer groups.

NOTES

1. Arnold Zellner, "An Efficient Method of Estimating Seemingly Unrelated Regression Equations", *Journal of American Statistical Association*, Vol. 517, 1962, pp. 348-68.
2. L.J. Lau and P.A. Yotopoulos, "A Test for Relative Efficiency and Application to Indian Agriculture", *American Economic Review*, Vol. 61, March 1971, pp. 94-109.
3. L.N. Dutta, "Relative Efficiency, Farm Size and Peasant Proprietorship: A Case Study of Ranchi District (Bihar)", *Indian Journal of Agricultural Economics*, Vol. 37, No. 1, January-March 1982, pp. 76-82.
4. C.H. Hanumantha Rao, *Technological Change and the Distribution of Gain in Indian Agriculture*, Macmillan Company of India Ltd., Delhi, 1975.

5. G. Subramaniyan, *Cotton in Madurai District: An Econometric Analysis*, Northern Book Centre, New Delhi, 1987.
6. Mahmood H. Khan and Dennis R. Maki, "Effects of Farm Size on Economic Efficiency: The Case of Pakistan", *American Journal of Agricultural Economics*, Vol. 61, 1979, pp. 64-69.
7. K. Kalirajan, "Testing Hypothesis of Equal Relative Economic Efficiency Using Restricted Aitken's Least Squares Estimation", *Journal of Development Studies*, Vol. 17, No. 4, July 1981, pp. 307-16.
8. V. Rajagopalan, "North Arcot, Tamil Nadu", *Changes in Rice Farming in Selected Areas of Asia*, International Rice Research Institute, Philippines, 1975, pp. 71-91.
9. K. Kalirajan, "The Economic Efficiency of Farmers Growing High-Yielding, Irrigated Rice in India", *American Journal of Agricultural Economics*, Vol. 66, No. 3, August 1981, pp. 566-70.
10. G. Parthasarthy and D.S. Prasad, "Response to the Impact of the New Rice Technology by Farm Size and Tenure — Andhra Pradesh", Interpretive Analysis of Selected Papers from *Changes in Rice Farming in Selected Areas of Asia*, IRRI, Philippines, 1978, pp. 11-27.

9

SUMMARY OF MAJOR FINDINGS AND POLICY IMPLICATIONS

Rice is the most important food crop of Tamil Nadu state. There are 20 districts in the state, of which Madurai is one. Gokilapuram is one of the most progressive rice producing villages of Uthamapalayam taluk in the district. More than 94 per cent of the total cropped area in the village was under rice cultivation in 1985-86. Considering the high level of adoption of high-yielding varieties of rice and technology, Gokilapuram was particularly chosen for a study on the economics of the cultivation of two popular rice varieties, viz., IR 20 and CO 37, in the village.

Of the 300 rice growers in the study area, majority of them cultivated IR 20 variety while only 54 farmers grew CO 37 variety in rabi, 1985-86. A random sample of 100 farmers were selected for a study on IR 20 variety. The sample farmers were classified into small and large farmer groups. Those cultivating an area of five acres and more were grouped under the large farmers category, while those cultivating less than five acres of land were classed as small farmers. There were 74 small and 26 large farmers in the sample. In the case of CO 37 variety (dropping out four farmers for the reason of their negligible size of operational holdings), 50 farmers were chosen for the study. Since the small size of sample did not facilitate their classification into the two groups of farmers, they were studied in total. Data for the study were collected during the rabi season of the agricultural year 1985-86.

A comprehensive study of the cost and return structure of the two rice varieties and of IR 20 farmer groups, determinants of their yields, yield gap and yield constraints, farm size and productivity, distribution of farm income, supply and demand elasticities and labour absorption and economic efficiency of IR 20 farmer groups was undertaken. The major findings and the important policy implications derived on the basis on the empirical analysis are presented in this chapter.

A study of the input and output structure of the two varieties of rice showed that IR 20 growers obtained significantly larger yield per acre than the CO 37 farmers. It speaks for the greater popularity of IR 20 variety over CO 37 in Gokilapuram and in Tamil Nadu in general.

A comparison of the levels of input use per acre by the cultivators of the two varieties revealed almost a similar pattern with respect to all inputs, except chemical fertilizer. The cultivation of IR 20 rice required a higher level of fertilizer application due to its greater responsiveness to the input.

Next, the levels of inputs used and output obtained per acre on small and large farms cultivating IR 20 rice were compared. A significant difference in the yield per acre was observed between the two sets of farmers. The level of inputs use per acre was higher on small farms. Small operators used significantly greater levels of bullock labour, human labour and pesticides. The more intensive use of bullock labour could be due to the ownership of bullock pairs, which enabled them to use it as much as required. The difference in human labour may be attributed to the active participation of family members on small farms. The higher level of pesticides application could be as a protection against pest-attack and assurance of a good yield. A small farmer is likely to have a greater interest in maximising his farm output than the large farmer, as a considerable proportion of the food crop is produced for self-consumption and only the surplus is marketed. Further, rice cultivation normally needs a quite close supervision which is easier on small farms. A small farmer is more likely to have an intimate knowledge of his farm land and its requirements. These help to increase the production efficiency on small farms.

The labour absorption capacity of IR 20 and CO 37 varieties was examined in the light of the following farm activities involved in rice cultivation: (i) preparatory cultivation, (ii) sowing and trans-plantation, (iii) application of organic manure and inorganic fertilizers, (iv) plant protection measure, (v) weeding, (vi) irrigation, (vii) harvesting, and (viii) threshing. An assessment of the number of male and female labourers employed and the payments made to them were studied separately.

Rice cultivation in general was found to be labour intensive in the study area. This suggests that cultivation of high-yielding varieties at large can help to provide gainful employment to the rural population for most of the year. Apart from creating additional employment in weeding, harvesting, etc., the shorter-duration of these varieties also help to increase the cropping intensities.

The composition of male and female labour employment per acre was almost similar for the two varieties. However, the cultivators of CO 37 variety incurred relatively higher labour cost compared to IR 20 farmers. Female labourers were paid lower than their male counterparts for the same work done. Besides, female labour was preferred for almost all farm activities, except preparatory cultivation, plant protection measures and irrigation. Activities of weeding, harvesting and sowing and transplanting required the maximum number of labourers, which incidentally, were all done by women. The employment of women workers for most of the farm activities could be due to the nature of the work and their relative cheapness in the labour market.

A comparative study of the pattern of male and female labour employment per acre by small and large IR 20 farmers revealed nearly an identical pattern. Women were employed for most of the farm activities, with the maximum number being engaged for sowing and transplanting, weeding and harvesting. The wages paid to labourers by the two farmer groups were almost the same. Female labour was paid considerably lower than their male counterpart. This may be one reason for the greater preference for female labour for most of the farm activities. The nature of agricultural activities may be another reason for their larger employment.

The cost and return structure of the two rice varieties revealed that the physical and monetary yield per acre of IR 20 variety was significantly larger than that of the CO 37 variety. The profit per acre from IR 20 rice cultivation was also considerably higher. This explains the greater preference for the variety among rice farmers not only in the village, but also at the state level.

The cost of cultivation per acre for IR 20 rice was comparatively higher, emphasising the need for a more intensive use of inputs for its farming. Variable cost formed about 70 per cent of the total cost in both cases. Human labour constituted the major cost component, accounting for more than 37 per cent of the total cost. This reflects the labour intensive nature of these high-yielding varieties of rice. Rent was the next prominent cost item. The expenditure on rent, chemical fertilizer and farm manure differed significantly between the two varieties. The difference in the application of chemical fertilizer and farm manure arose out of the greater responsiveness of IR 20 variety to the inputs. The difference in rent within the same area may be due to the imperfections in land market. The pattern of other input expenditures was almost similar for the two varieties.

A comparison of the cost and return structure of the IR 20 farmer groups showed that the yield per acre of small operators was significantly larger than that of the large operators. This may be due to the more intensive use of inputs and better personal supervision and farm management on small farms. However, it was the large farmer group who received greater monetary return per acre. The net income was significantly higher for the large farmers. Distress sales of grains immediately after harvest due to tied loans, lack of storage facilities, etc., may be the cause for the disposal of the marketable surplus by small farmers when conditions are unprofitable. The better economic and social status of large farmers enable them to wait and sell their produce at relatively higher prices.

The cost of cultivation incurred by small farmers was considerably greater, indicating intensive cultivation to ensure good returns. The pattern of input expenditure per acre for the two sets of farmers was similar. Variable cost constituted about 70 per cent of the total cost. Expenditure on human labour was the most important cost item, followed by rent. Expenditure on human labour, bullock labour, pesticides and rent differed significantly between the two farmer groups. The difference in expenditure on human labour arises out of the greater employment of family labour by the small farmers. The expenditure on bullock labour was also high on small farms due to owned bullock pairs, which are used intensively. Greater expenditure on pesticides could be as a protection against pest-attack to ensure a good yield, which would cater to the needs of self-consumption and marketable surplus. The difference in rent within the same village may be explained by the imperfections in land market.

An examination of the economics of rice cultivation in Gokilapuram showed that cultivation of IR 20 variety would be more profitable to rice farmers at large. Although the cost of cultivation per acre was higher for IR 20 variety, its returns in terms of physical and monetary units were remarkably higher than for the CO 37 variety. This accounts for the greater popularity of the IR 20 variety over more than 20 years of its release, despite the subsequent introduction of more location-specific and shorter-duration varieties in the following years. This may also be because the farmers are more accustomed to cultivating it. Hence, their reluctance to cultivate any other new variety, however better, to avoid risk and uncertainties and to have an assured market.

A comparative analysis of the economics of IR 20 rice cultivation by the two sets of farmers revealed that although the small operators reaped a larger yield per acre incurring a higher cost of cultivation, it was the large operators who enjoyed substantially greater benefits. This may be due to the better social and economic position of the large farmers who are able to wait longer and procure maximum price for their produce at the market. In this respect, strict and proper functioning of the existing government institutions such as regulated markets, credit societies and other cooperative societies can play a remarkable role by discharging their duties at the time of need, for the right section of farmers. This would help to improve the economic standards of small farmers to a great extent and ameliorate the problems of middlemen, money-lenders, etc.

A Cobb-Douglas form of multiple regression model was fitted to identify the major determinants of yield of IR 20 and CO 37 rice and that of IR 20 small and large farmer groups in Gokilapuram. The five independent variables chosen to explain the variations in rice yield were: (i) human labour, (ii) fertilizer, (iii) pesticides, (iv) capital flows, and (v) net return of the previous harvest.

In the case of IR 20 rice, the five independent variables jointly explained about 55 per cent of the variations in rice yield. All the explanatory variables, except human labour, were positively and significantly related to yield. Net return was the most important determinant of yield. It was followed by capital flows, fertilizer and pesticides. The regression model emerged highly significant.

The regression analysis for CO 37 variety revealed that the independent variables caused about 90 per cent of the variations in the yield per acre. All the five factors exercised positive influence on the dependent variable. Human labour and capital flows were significantly related to yield. Human labour was the most influential variable in the determination of CO 37 rice yield. It was followed by pesticides, net return and other factors. The regression model was statistically significant at five per cent level. The emergence of human labour as an important determinant of yield indicated that intensive use of the input had a salutary effect on increasing its yield.

In order to investigate whether structural difference existed between the farmers cultivating IR 20 and CO 37 rice varieties, Chow test was adopted. The analysis based on dummy variables revealed the existence of structural difference between the two rice farmers, at both the slope and intercept levels. At the intercept level, the varietal difference of the two rice caused the differences in yield between the two varieties. At the slope level, variable factors human labour, fertilizer, pesticides and net return were responsible for the differences in their yields.

The study on the determinants of yield of IR 20 large and small farmers showed that the two regression models were statistically significant. Of the five independent variables, net return was the most important determinant of yield, followed by fertilizer and capital flows. The importance of net return emphasised the role of economic incentive as an important stimuli to increase yield. The coefficient of fertilizer indicated the greater responsiveness of the variety to the input. The regression models for the two farmer groups emerged highly significant. The analysis based on Chow-test revealed that there was no structural difference between the two groups of farmers.

The analysis of yield gap revealed the existence of a gap between the potential and actual yield per acre under both varieties. The yield gap under IR 20 variety emerged larger compared to CO 37 variety.

Of the various yield constraints, the selected farmers listed three bio-physical (water shortage, insects and weeds) and three socio-economic factors (credit, non-availability of inputs when required and traditional methods) to be the major constraints to the attainment of potential yield in the study area. Majority of the farmers cultivating the two rice varieties reported insects and water shortage to be the main constraints to maximum yield. It was followed by the other factors. This suggested that yield gap in Gokilapuram may be over-come by breaking the bottlenecks limiting yield increases at farm level. This calls for strict implementation of the existing programmes relating to the specific problems stated by the farmers. Active extension services can help the farmers to give up the traditional methods, which restrict them from attaining the potential yield. This would enable all farmers to enjoy the benefit of maximum yield under the new agricultural technology.

The nature of relationship between farm size and productivity was investigated using simple linear regression models, with respect to the two rice varieties. In the case of both IR 20 and CO 37 rice cultivation, the relationship between farm size and output per acre was negative and statistically significant in the study area. This indicated a decline in productivity, in response to an increase in acreage. This may be because, as the area under cultivation increases, factors like managerial skill and other input application get spread over a larger area, thus reducing their production efficiency.

A significant and inverse relationship was identified between average variable cost and acreage and average cost and acreage under both varieties. This behaviour may be explained by economies of scale, which sets-in with the expansion in farm size. Almost all the regression models (except output per manday and acreage) were statistically significant at five per cent level.

Inequalities in income distribution from the cultivation of the two rice varieties was examined using Gini coefficient. The Gini coefficient of net income was 0.159 for IR 20 variety and 0.121 for CO 37. It revealed that inequalities in income distribution from the cultivation of IR 20 rice was slightly greater compared to CO 37 rice. A comparison of the two Gini coefficients using the variances of logarithms of IR 20 and CO 37 varieties showed that there was no significant difference in the degree of inequality in income distribution between the two rice varieties.

The analysis on output supply and labour demand elasticities revealed that the two farmer groups in Gokilapuram were not so responsive to changes in rice price. The finding confirms Mellor's hypothesis that output price does not have much effect on its supply. This indicated that manipulation of rice price may not be very effective in increasing output supply. This is encouraging from the national point of view, which aims at raising consumers' welfare at large. As far as the impact of rice price on labour demand is concerned, a 10 per cent increase in rice price was observed to increase labour demand by more than 10 per cent under the two varieties. The demand for labour with regard to real wage rate was elastic in both cases. This implied that a 10 per cent reduction in wage rate could increase labour employment by more than 10 per cent in the study area. However, wage cut is not a practicable solution in the face of active labour unions, which may strongly oppose such an action. Therefore, if the policy-makers aim at increasing employment, output price policy appears to be a more suitable tool. However, it should be framed by taking into account all socio-economic consequences.

The negative and low responsiveness of output supply and labour demand to increase in the prices of fertilizer, pesticides and bullock pair indicated that manipulation of factor prices is not an effective policy measure. A greater reduction in the prices of these inputs may be necessary to stimulate output supply. Increase in area under rice had a favourable effect on increasing rice supply and labour demand. On the other hand, an impact of changes in capital flows was quite negligible.

A study on the demand for variable inputs in response to changes in their own prices for the two rice varieties indicated that a 10 per cent increase in the prices of these factors was likely to be followed by a more than 10 per cent decrease in their demands. Thus in both cases, the demand for variable inputs was highly elastic. Among the variable inputs, real wage was relatively the most important factor influencing farm employment to a considerable extent.

The cross price elasticities of the inputs were negative and low in all cases, indicating that these variables were complements rather than substitutes of each other. However in the case of CO 37, the cross price elasticities of fertilizer implied that the inputs were substitutes. This appears to be illogical. Nevertheless, the magnitudes of the cross price elasticities being quite low, they may be ignored.

The indirect estimates for the two rice varieties revealed that land (63 per cent in IR 20 and 78 per cent in CO 37) and labour (22 per cent each) were the dominant factors of production. The shares of other factors were quite low under both the varieties. The positive value of fertilizer for IR 20 and negative value for CO 37 could be due to the greater responsiveness of the former variety to this input. The low production elasticities of pesticides, highlighted the pest-resistant characteristic of the modern rice varieties. In both cases, there was an evidence of constant returns to scale. This ruled out the policy of consolidation of land holdings in Gokilapuram.

Based on the analysis of the relative economic efficiency of the two farmer groups cultivating IR 20 rice, the hypothesis of equal economic efficiency of small and large farmers was rejected. The result showed that small farmers were economically more efficient than large farmers. This may be due to the more intensive use of inputs by them. The smaller size of their operational holdings further facilitates better personal supervision and farm management. It may thus be inferred that, given the same access to factors of production, small farmers were more efficient in maximising profits. In order to identify the sources of difference in economic efficiency (price/ technical) of the two sets of farmers, *F*-test was used.

The test of equal relative price efficiency of the two farmer groups showed that the hypothesis of equal price efficiency was rejected. The study indicated that the two farmer groups were able to equate marginal value product with marginal cost with respect to all inputs, except fertilizer. In order words, fertilizer was a disturbing factor in their decision-making, which prevented the two groups from maximising profits to the same degree in the study area. This may be because the sample farmers applied fertilizer lower than the profit maximising choice, due to risk aversion and uncertainty.

The hypothesis of equal technical efficiency between the two farmer groups was also rejected at five per cent level. Small farmers emerged technically more efficient than large farmers. This could be due to the better supervision and farm management favoured by the smaller size of operational holdings. This indicated that apart from proper input application, direct supervision and farm management are crucial determinants of economic efficiency. Further, it is suggested that extension service officials may improve technical efficiency by advicing the farmers on input application at proper time, as recommended.

APPENDIX

QUESTIONNAIRE

An Economic Analysis of Rice Cultivation: A Study of Tamil Nadu

No. ———

Supervisor: Dr. G. Subramaniyan Researcher: Ms V. Nirmala
Madurai Kamaraj University

1.1 PARTICULARS ON HOUSEHOLD:

1. Name of the Head of the Household :
2. Sex :
3. Age :
4. Address :
5. Occupation :
6. Religion and Caste :
7. Education :
8. Experience in Rice Cultivation :

1.2 FAMILY MEMBERS AND THEIR OCCUPATION:

Sl. No.	Name	Age	Education in years	Relationship to Head	Main Occupation	Subsidiary Occupation	Work Place	Annual Non-Agri. Income in Rs.

2.1 FARM SIZE HOLDING UNDER RICE IN 1985-86:

Particular	Size in Acres	Soil Type	Water Quality	Present Value in Rupees	Rental Value in Rupees per Annum
A. Land Details:					
(a) Area owned					
(b) Area leased-in					
(c) Area leased-out					
(d) Operational holding					
B. Land Revenue, Taxes, etc.					

3.1 FARM INVENTORY

Particular	Year of Purchase/ Construction	Value at the Time of Purchase/ Construction	Life Expected	Present Value in Rs.	Maintenance Cost Per Year
A. Building & Structure:					
(a) Farm house (dwelling-cum-storage)					
(b) Cattle shed					
(c) Pump shed					
(d) Tractor shed					
(e) Storage					
(f) Threshing floor					
B. Wells & Irrigation Structure:					
(a) Open well					
(b) Bore well					
(c) Irrigation channel					
C. Livestock in Number:					
1.					
2.					
3.					
4.					

3.2 DEAD STOCK:

Particulars	H.P.Nos.	Year of Purchase /Construction	Value at the Time of Purchase/Construction	Life Expected	Present Value in Rs.	Maintenance Cost Per Year
(a) Tractor						
(b) Pumpset with						
(i) Oil engine						
(ii) Electric motor						
(c) Sprayers						
(i) Hand operated						
(ii) Power operated						
(d) Conventional						
(i) Levellers						
(ii) Bund formers						
(iii) Country plough						
(iv) Bullock cart						
(v) Others						

4.1 PERMANENT HIRED LABOUR:

Sl. No.	Name	Sex	Age	Educational Qualification	Man-days Worked	Wage Bill per Annum			
						Kind		Cash in Rs	Total
						Qty.	Value		

4.2 FAMILY LABOUR:

Sl. No.	Name	Sex	Age	Educational Qualification	Mandays Worked	Opportunity Cost in Rs.	Total

4.3 PROPORTION OF FAMILY LABOUR TO TOTAL LABOUR: ——————

5.1 PREPARATORY CULTIVATION:

Sl. No.	Operation	No. of Bullock Pair	Hire Charges per Pair	Expenditure on Bullock Pair	No. of		Wage Rate in Rs.		Total Wages in Rs.
					Male	Female	Male	Female	
1.	Ploughing								
2.	Ploughing								
3.	Ploughing								
4.	Ploughing								
5.	Levelling								
6.	Rectification of Bunds, etc.								

Total Expenses in Rs. ——————

5.2 SEEDS AND SOWING:

Sl. No.	Variety	Source	Quantity in kg.	Price per kg.	Value in Rs.	Certified/ Non-certified	No. of		Wage Rate		Total Cost
							M.L.	F.L.	M.L.	F.L.	

Total Expenses in Rs. ——————

5.3 TRANSPLANTATION:

Sl. No.	Number of		Wage in				Value per Unit	Total Cost in Rs.
	M.L.	F.L.	Cash (Rs.)		Kind (Qty.)			
			M.L.	F.L.	M.L.	F.L.		

Total Cost in Rs. ———

5.4 ORGANIC MANURE:

Sl. No.	No. of Cart Load (C.L.)	C.L.	Cost per C.L.	No. of		Wage Rate	Application Cost in Rs.	Total Cost in Rs.	Remarks
				M.L.	F.L.				

Total Cost in Rs. ———

5.5 INORGANIC FERTILIZERS:

Sl. No.	Fertilizer Used	Qty. in kgs.	Components of N.P.K.	Price per kg.	Value in Rs.	No. of		Wage Rate		Total Application Charges in Rs.	Total Cost	Remarks
						M.L.	F.L.	M.L.	F.L.			

Total Cost in Rs. ——

5.6 WEEDING:

Sl. No.	No. of Hand Weeding	No. of		Wage Rate		Total Cost in Rs.	Remarks
		M.L.	F.L.	M.L.	F.L.		

Total Cost in Rs. ——

5.7 PLANT PROTECTION MEASURES:

Sl. No.	Chemical used	Qty. used	Price per Unit	Value in Rs.	Area Sprayed	Rent for Spr./Dtr.	Fuel Charges	Application charge per Tank	No. of Tanks	Application Cost	Total Cost in Rs.

Total Cost in Rs. ———

5.8 TOTAL IRRIGATION COST: Rs. ———

5.9 HARVESTING:

Date of Harvest ———

Sl. No.	No. of		Wages in				Value Per Unit	Total Labour Cost in Rs.	Qty. of Rice Harvested in kg.	Remarks
			Cash (Rs.)		Kind (Qty.)					
	M.L.	F.L.	M.L.	F.L.	M.L.	F.L.				

Total Cost in Rs. ———

5.10 THRESHING

Sl. No.	No. of		Wages in				Value Per Unit	Total Labour Cost in Rs.	Qty. of Rice Harvested	Remarks
			Cash (Rs.)		Kind (Qty.)					
	M.L.	F.L.	M.L.	F.L.	M.L.	F.L.				

Total Cost in Rs. ——

Marketing Cost Rs. ——

6.1 PROBLEMS FACED BY THE FARMERS IN MARKETING RICE:

Sl. No.	Date	Qty. sold in Quintals	Selling price per Quintal	Place of Sale	To whom it was Sold	Reason for Preference	Cleaning	Packing	Trans-port	Market Fee	Commiss-ion	Others Amount	Net Amo-unt

Total Amount in Rs. ——

6.2 CREDIT:

Have you taken loan for rice crop? YES/NO

If yes:

Source	Date of Borrowing	Amount Borro-wed in Rs.	From whom Borrowed	Reason for Preference	Rate of Interest	Duration	Security	Amount Repaid	Amount Outstanding

6.3 INPUTS AVAILABILITY RATES:

Have you applied the recommended doses of inputs? YES/NO

If no, Why?

Constraints in:

(a) Farm finance
(b) Lack of extension services
(c) Non-availability of vital inputs like power, water, etc.
(d) Others

6.4 Do you receive the necessary extension services regularly? YES/NO

If no, What are the constraints?

6.4 YIELD:

Have you obtained the maximum possible yield? YES/NO

If No:

(a) What is the maximum possible yield?
(b) What is the quantity produced by you?
(c) Difference: Quantity .... % to maximum.
(d) What are the reasons for the difference?

Rank the following reasons as per priority.

Reasons:

Bio-Physical		Remedy	Socio-Economic		Remedy
(i)	Water control		(viii)	Credit	
(ii)	Soil fertility		(ix)	Input availability	
(iii)	Problems of the soil		(x)	Economic behaviour	
(iv)	Insects		(xi)	Risk version	
(v)	Weeds		(xii)	Knowledge	
(vi)	Variety		(xiii)	Institutions	
(vii)	Cultural practices		(xiv)	Traditions	

7.1 Is your crop affected by any plant disease? YES/NO

If Yes:

(i) Mention the disease ——————
(ii) Pesticides used ——————

Name of the Investigator:

Date of Survey

BIBLIOGRAPHY

A. Books

Bansil, P.C., *Agricultural Problems of India*, Oxford and IBH Publishing Co., New Delhi, 1981.

Bliss, C.J. and N.H. Stern, *Palanpur: The Economy of an Indian Village*, Oxford University Press, Delhi, 1982.

Garrett, Henry E. and R.S. Woodworth, *Statistics in Psychology and Education*, Vakils, Feffer and Simons Ltd., Bombay, 1981.

Goldberger, A.S., *Econometric Theory*, John Wiley and Sons, Inc., New York, 1964.

Gujarati, Damodar, *Basic Econometrics*, McGraw-Hill, New Delhi, 1978.

Johnston, J., *Econometric Methods*, McGraw-Hill Book Company, New York, 1972.

Hanumantha Rao, C.H., *Technological Change and Distribution of Gains in Indian Agriculture*, Macmillan Company of India Ltd., Delhi, 1975.

Kahlon, A.S. and Karam Singh, *Economics of Farm Management in India: Theory and Practice*, Allied Publishers Pvt. Ltd., New Delhi, 1981.

Kahlon, A.S. and D.S. Tyagi, *Agricultural Price Policy in India*, Allied Publishers Pvt. Ltd., New Delhi, 1983.

Kmenta, J., *Elements of Econometrics*, Macmillan, London, 1971.

Mathew, K.M. (Ed.), *Manorama Year Book*, Manorama Publishing House, Kerala, 1987.

Misra, S.K. and V.K. Puri, *Indian Economy*, Himalaya Publishing House, Delhi, 1986.

Pearse, Andrew, *Seeds of Plenty, Seeds of Want — Social and Economic Implications of the Green Revolution*, Clarendon Press, Oxford, 1980.

Poduval, R.N., *Foodgrain Economy of Tamil Nadu: Problems and Prospects*, Emerald Publishers, Madras, 1987.

Ranadive, K.R., *Income Distribution: The Unsolved Puzzle*, Oxford University Press, Bombay, 1978.

Rayachaudhuri, S.P. (Ed.), *Advances in Indian Agriculture*, Vol. 1, Books and Periodicals Agency, New Delhi, 1983.

Richharia, R.H. and S. Govindasamy, *Rice in India*, Central Rice Research Institute, Scientific Book Company, Cuttack, 1966.

Sadhu, A.N. and R.K. Mahajan, *Technological Change and Agricultural Development in India*, Himalaya Publishing House, Delhi, 1985.

Saini, G.R., *Farm Size, Resource Use Efficiency and Income Distribution*, Allied Publishers Pvt. Ltd., New Delhi, 1979.

Singh, J.P. and Others, *New Seeds: Adoption and Yield*, Sterling Publishers Pvt. Ltd., New Delhi, 1979.

Stubb, R.W., et al., *Cereal Disease Methodology Manual*, CIMMYT, Mexico, 1986.

Subramaniyan, G., *Cotton in Madurai District: An Econometric Analysis*, Northern Book Centre, New Delhi, 1987.

Theil, H., *Economics and Information Theory*, North Holland Publishing Company, Amsterdam, 1967.

B. Journals

Aiyasamy, P.K., V. Rajagopalan and R. Sundaresan, "Economic Appraisal of Pattern of Labour Utilisation in Different Tracts of Tamil Nadu", *Southern Economic Review*, Vol. 5, No. 1, July 1975, pp. 31-49.

Anderson, J.R. and N.S. Jodha, "On Cobb-Douglas and Related Myths", *Economic and Political Weekly*, Review of Agriculture, Vol. VIII, June 1973, pp. A-65–A-75.

Bisaliah, S., "Decomposition Analysis of Employment Change under New Production Technology in Punjab Agriculture", *Indian Journal of Agricultural Economics*, Vol. 33, No. 2, April-June 1978, pp. 70-80.

Byres, T., "Dialectics of Green Revolution", *South Asia Review*, Vol. 5, No. 2, 1972, pp. 99-116.

Chattopadhyay, M. and Ashok Rudra, "Size-Productivity Revisited", *Economic and Political Weekly*, Review of Agriculture, Vol. XI, No. 39, September 25, 1976, pp. A-104–A-116.

——, "Size-Productivity Revisited", *Economic and Political Weekly*, Vol. XII, No. 11, March 12, 1977, pp. 476-84.

Chaudhary, F.S. and H.C. Sharma, "Research Strategy and Dynamics of Rice Production in India", *Economic Affairs*, Vol. 27, Nos.1-3, January-March 1982, pp. 324-44.

Chow, Gregory C., "Tests of Equality between Sets of Coefficients in Two Linear Regressions", *Econometrica*, Vol. 28, No. 3, July 1960, pp. 591-605.

Davidson, B.R. and B.R. Martin, "The Relationship between Yields on Farms and in Experiments", *Australian Journal of Agricultural Economics*, Vol. 9, No. 2, December 1965, pp. 129-40.

Desai, D.K., "Intensive Agricultural District Programme", *Economic and Political Weekly*, Review of Agriculture, Vol. IV, No. 2, June 1969, pp. A-83–A-90.

Dutta, L.N. "Relative Efficiency, Farm Size and Peasant Proprietorship – A Case Study of Ranchi District (Bihar)", *Indian Journal of Agricultural Economics*, Vol. 37, No. 1, January-March 1982, pp. 76-82.

Flinn, J.C., K. Kalirajan and Linda L. Castillo, "Supply Responsiveness of Rice Farmers in Laguna, Philippines", *Australian Journal of Agricultural Economics*, Vol. 26, No. 1, April 1982, pp. 39-48.

Flinn, J.C. and Mubarak Ali, "Technical Efficiency in Basmati Rice Production", *Pakistan Journal of Applied Economics*, Vol. 5, No. 1, 1986, pp. 1-22.

Fujimoto, Akimi, "Farm Management Analysis of Malay and Chinese Rice Farming in Province of Wellesley, Malaysia", *Journal of Developing Economies*, Vol. XI, No. 1, March 1983, pp. 35-50.

Ghosh, Madhusudan, "Farm Size Productivity Nexus under Alternative Technology", *Indian Journal of Agricultural Economics*, Vol. 41, No. 1, January-March 1986, pp. 17-28.

Hanumantha Rao, C.H., "Alternative Explanation of the Inverse Relationship between Farm Size and Output per Acre in India", *Indian Economic Review*, (New Series), Vol. 1, No. 2, October 1966, pp. 1-2.

Haque, T., "Temporal and Regional Variations in the Agrarian Structure in India", *Indian Journal of Agricultural Economics*, Vol. 42, No. 3, July-September 1987, pp. 313-18.

Junankar, P.N., "Do Indian Farmers Maximise Profits", *Journal of Development Studies*, Vol. 17, No. 1, October 1980, pp. 48-61.

Kalirajan, K., "Benefits from the High-Yielding Varieties Programme and their Distribution in an Irrigated Paddy Area",

Indian Journal of Agricultural Economics, Vol. 35, No. 3, July-September 1980, pp. 70-76.

———, "The Contribution of Location Specific Research to Agricultural Productivity", *Indian Journal of Agricultural Economics*, Vol. 35, No. 4, October-December 1980, pp. 8-16.

———, "Testing the Hypothesis of Equal Relative Economic Efficiency Using Restricted Aitken's Least Squares Estimation", *Journal of Development Studies*, Vol. 17, No. 4, July 1981, pp. 307-316.

———, "The Economic Efficiency of Farmers Growing High Yielding, Irrigated Rice in India", *American Journal of Agricultural Economics*, Vol. 63, No. 3, August 1981, pp. 566-70.

Kalirajan, K. and J.C. Flinn, "Allocative Efficiency and Supply Response in Irrigated Rice Production", *Indian Journal of Agricultural Economics*, Vol. 36, No. 2, April-June 1981, pp. 16-24.

Kalirajan, K. and R.T. Shand, "Labour Absorption in Tamil Nadu Agriculture -- A Micro Analysis", *Journal of Developing Economies*, Vol. XX, No. 3, September 1981, pp. 333-43.

———, "Location Specific Research: Rice Technology in India", *Land Economics*, Vol. 58, No. 4, November 1982, pp. 537-46.

Khan, Mahmood H. and Dennis R. Maki, "Effects of Farm Size on Economic Efficiency: The Case of Pakistan", *American Journal of Agricultural Economics*, Vol. 61, February 1979, pp. 64-69.

Khusro, A.M. "Returns to Scale in Indian Agriculture", *Indian Journal of Agricultural Economics*, Vol. XIX, Nos.3&4, July-December 1964, pp. 51-80.

Lau, L.J. and P.A. Yotopoulos, "A Test for Relative Efficiency and Application to Indian Agriculture", *American Economic Review*, Vol. 61, March 1971, pp. 95-109.

———, "Profits, Supply and Factor Demand Functions", *American Journal of Agricultural Economics*, Vol. 54, No. 1, February 1972, pp. 11-18.

Mahajan, R.K., A.V. Rao and D. Gandhi, "Rice Production in India During 1970s", *Agricultural Situation in India*, Vol. XL, No. 1, February 1986, p.987.

Mehra, S., "Some Aspects of Labour Use in Indian Agriculture", *Indian Journal of Agricultural Economics*, Vol. 31, No. 4, October-December 1976, pp. 95-125.

Nirmala, V. and G. Subramaniyan, "Yield Gap Analysis in Rice Cultivation: A Case Study", *Southern Economist*, Vol. 27, No. 15, December 1,1988, pp. 15-16.

——— "Input Demand and Output Supply Response of Rice Farmers in Gokilapuram, Tamil Nadu (India)", *The Indian Journal of Economics*, Vol. LXXI, Part II, No. 281, October 1990, pp. 163-174.

Panghal, B.S., R.N. Pandey and A.C. Gangwar, "An Analysis of Attainable Yield Gap in Important Foodgrain Crops in Haryana", *Agricultural Situation in India*, Vol. XL, No. 1, April 1985, pp. 7-12.

Quiggin, John and Anh Bui-Lan, "The Use of Cross-Sectional Estimates of Profit Function for Tests of Relative Efficiency: A Critical Review", *Australian Journal of Agricultural Economics*, Vol. 28, No. 1, April 1984, pp. 44-55.

Raj, K.N., "Some Questions Concerning Growth: Transformation and Planning of Agriculture in Developing Countries", *Journal of Development Planning*, Vol. I, No. 1, 1969, pp. 15-38.

Rajkrishna, "Some Production Function for the Punjab", *Indian Journal of Agricultural Economics*, Vol. XIX, Nos. 3&4, July-December 1964, pp. 87-97.

Rani, Usha, "Size of Farm and Productivity", *Economic and Political Weekly*, Vol. VI, No. 26, June 26, 1971, pp. A-85–A-89.

Rudra, Ashok and M.M. Mukhopadyay, "Hiring of Labour by Poor Peasants", *Economic and Political Weekly*, Vol. 11, Nos. 1&2, 10th January 1976, pp. 33-36.

Rudra, Ashok and A.K. Sen, "Farm Size and Labour Use: Analysis and Policy", *Economic and Political Weekly*, Annual No. , Vol. XV, Nos. 5, 6 & 7, February 1980, pp. 391-94.

Saini, G.R., "Holding Size, Productivity and Some Related Aspects of Indian Agriculture", *Economic and Political Weekly*, Vol. VI, No. 26, June 26, 1971, pp. A-79–A-85.

———, "Green Revolution and Disparities in Farm Income – A Comment", *Economic and Political Weekly*, Vol. XI, No. 46, November 13, 1976, pp. 1804-1806.

Sen, A.K., "Size of Holding and Productivity", *Economic Weekly*, Annual No. , Vol. XVI, Nos. 5, 6 & 7, February 1964.

Sharma, R.K., "Green Revolution and Farm Employment: An Analysis of Experience in Punjab", *Indian Journal of Industrial Relations*, Vol. 10, No. 2, October 1974.

Subramaniyan, G., "Labour Demand and Supply Responsiveness of Cotton in Madurai District", *Indian Journal of Agricultural Economics*, Vol. 41, No. 2, April-June 1986, pp. 155-63.

Yotopoulos, P.A. and L.J. Lau, "A Test for Relative Economic Efficiency – Some Further Results", *American Economic Review*, Vol. 63, No. 3, 1973, pp. 214-23.

Zellner, Arnold, "An Efficient Method for Estimating Seemingly Unrelated Regressions and Tests of Aggregation Bias", *Journal of the American Statistical Association*, Vol. 57, No. 2, June 1962, pp. 348-75.

C. Reports

"Agriculture and Allied Activities", *Tamil Nadu – An Economic Appraisal: 1985-86*, Evaluation and Applied Research Department, Madras 1987.

Brady, N.C. (Ed.), *Constraints to High Yields on Asian Rice Farms: An Interim Report*, International Rice Research Institute, Philippines, October 1977.

Brady, N.C. (Ed.), *Farm-Level Constraints to High Rice Yields in Asia, 1974-77*, International Rice Research Institute, Philippines, 1979.

Crop Production Guide, Horticulture and Oilseeds, Tamil Nadu Agricultural University and Directorate of Agriculture, TNAU, Coimbatore, 1985.

Johl, S.S., *Mechanization, Labour Use and Productivity in Indian Agriculture*, Ohio State University, U.S.A., 1974.

Lim, D., *Supply Responses of Primary Producers*, Penerbit University, Malaya, Kuala Lumpur, 1975.

Mellor, J.W., "Determinants of Rural Poverty: The Dynamics of Production, Technology and Price", *Agricultural Change and Rural Poverty* (Eds.) J.W. Mellor and G.M. Desai, Food Policy Research Institute, Washington, D.C., 1985, pp. 21-40.

Parthasarthy, G. and D.S. Prasad, *Spatial Variations in Rates of Growth of Productivity of Rice: An Analysis of 'Top' and 'Bottom' Districts*, Department of Cooperative and Applied Economics, Andhra Pradesh University, Waltair, 1977.

Rajagopalan, V. and Others, *Studies on Cost of Production of Major Crops in Tamil Nadu*, Department of Agricultural Economics, Tamil Nadu Agricultural University, Coimbatore, 1978.

Rajasekaran, S., *Distinguishing Morphological Features of Rabi Rice Varieties*, State Level Training Programme on Rice Production Technology, Agricultural College and Research Institute, TNAU, Madurai, 19th-22nd November, 1984.

Swaminathan, M.S., Lecture, *The Hindu*, 19th March 1983, in "Bridging Gap in Yields between Average Farms and Research Centres", *Monthly Reporter*, Director of Agriculture, Madras, Vol. 9, No. 5, October 1983, pp. 1-6.

Swaminathan, Madhura, *Credit for Rural Development in Southern Tamil Nadu*, Tamil Nadu Agricultural University, September 1986.

Yotopoulos, P.A. and L.J. Lau, *Resource Use in Agriculture: Application of the Profit Function to Selected Countries*, Food Research Institute Studies, Vol. XVII, No. 1, 1979.

D. Working Papers

Arputharaj, C., *Agricultural Development Potential in Tamil Nadu*, Summary of Lecture Delivered at the Department of Economics, Madurai Kamaraj University, Madurai, 16th February, 1983.

Cordova, V.C., *New Rice Technology: Its Effects on Labour Use and Shares in Rice Production in Laguna, Philippines*, Agricultural Economic Department Paper, No. 3002, International Rice Research Institute, Philippines, 1980.

Khan, M.H. and D.R. Maki, *Relative Efficiency by Farm Size and the Green Revolution in Pakistan*, Department of Economics and Commerce, Discussion Paper 77-91, Simon Fraser University, Canada, January 1974.

Kikuchi, M. and Others, *Technological Progress and Income Distribution in a Rice Village in West Java*, International Rice Research Institute, Research Paper Series No. 55, Philippines, December 1980.

Kikuchi, M., A. Huysman and L. Res, *New Rice Technology and Labour Absorption – Comparative Histories of Two Philippine Villages*, IRRI Research Paper Series, No. 90, Philippines, April 1983.

Mukherji, D.K., *Gap Analysis – An Effective Production Increase Concept in Rice*, Summary of Lecture Delivered at the State Level Training Meeting on Rice held at Purila, Department of Agriculture, West Bengal, India, July 1977.

Parthasarthy, G. and D.S. Prasad, "Response to the Impact of the New Rice Technology by Farm Size and Tenure – Andhra Pradesh", Interpretive Analysis of Selected Paper from *Changes in Rice Farming in Selected Areas of Asia*, International Rice Research Institute, Philippines, 1978, pp. 111-27.

Rajagopalan, V., "North Arcot, Tamil Nadu", *Changes in Rice Farming in Selected Areas of Asia*, International Rice Research Institute, Philippines, 1975, pp. 71-91.

Subramaniyan, G. and S. Chelladurai, *Farm Size, Returns to Scale and Absorption of Labour in Tamil Nadu Agriculture: A Micro Analysis*, Paper presented at 23rd All India Econometric Conference, Osmania University, Hyderabad, January 3-5, 1985.

Unnevehr, L.J. and M.L. Stanford, *Technology and the Demand for Women's Labour in Asian Rice Farming*, Paper presented at the Conference on Women in Rice Farming Systems, International Rice Research Institute, September 26-30, 1983.

E. Thesis

Harrison, James Quigley, Agricultural Modernization and Income Distribution: An Economic Analysis of the Impact of New Seed Varieties in the Crop Production of Large and Small Farms in India, (mimeo), Ph.D., Princeton University, 1972.

F. Sources of Secondary Data

Adangal, Village Account No. 2, Fasli Year 1395, Gokilapuram, 1985-86.

Census of India, Government of India Publication, New Delhi, 1981.

Commissioners of All Panchayat Unions, *District Statistical Hand Book for 1985-86*, Assistant Director of Statistics Office, Madurai, 1986.

Research Station Record, Tamil Nadu Agricultural University, Madurai, 1985-86.

Weather Report, Taluk Office, Uthamapalayam, Madurai, 1983-86.